# *stove-top*
# indian
## *cooking*

# stove-top indian cooking

## QUICK AND EASY BALTI STIR-FRIES

### SHEHZAD HUSAIN

LORENZ BOOKS

This edition first published in 2001 by Lorenz Books
27 West 20th Street, New York, NY 10011

LORENZ BOOKS are available for bulk purchase for sales promotion
and for premium use. For details, write or call the sales director,
Lorenz Books, 27 West 20th Street, New York, NY 10011

www.lorenzbooks.com

Lorenz Books is an imprint of
Anness Publishing Inc.

*Publisher:* Joanna Lorenz
*Project Editor:* Judith Simons
*Text Editor:* Kate Bell
*Designer:* David Rowley
*Photographer:* David Armstrong

*Front cover:* William Lingwood, Photographer;
Helen Trent, Stylist; Sunil Vijayakar, Home Economist

Previously published as part of the Creative Cooking Library Series, *The Balti Cookbook*

1  3  5  7  9  10  8  6  4  2

# Contents

# Introduction

BALTI cooking is something of a culinary phenomenon. Originally introduced to the West by Pakistan's resident Multani community some ten years ago, it was taken up, refined and adapted by enterprising restaurateurs with great success: specialist Balti curry houses are becoming very popular.

Balti is, essentially, a method of cooking a wide range of curries – poultry, fish, meat and vegetable dishes – quickly on the stove-top over a high heat using a stir-fry technique. The generally better known 'karahi' cuisine is already firmly established in the culinary vernacular of Indian and Pakistani food enthusiasts. Karahi, literally meaning a wok-shaped cooking vessel with ring handles on either side, is extensively used in Pakistan and India for all types of deep-frying, especially for bhajias, samosas and sweets like jalebi. Karahis come in varying sizes from the very large commercial type, which is almost mandatory in every Pakistani and Indian street-side café where the chef displays his cooking skills just outside or by the restaurant entrance, to the smaller variety in which individual portions are cooked and served at the restaurant table, and which is now so familiar to curry lovers in the West.

Pakistan is the home of a rich and varied cuisine, drawing on the influences of its neighbours Afghanistan, Iran and India to augment its own traditional dishes. In addition, through the course of history, the dishes of the Mongols, Arabs and even the Greeks have been absorbed into Pakistan's culinary repertoire. Balti is one such type of cooking, which has its roots in northern Pakistan but which incorporates many influences, not least those of the cuisine's popularizers in the West.

Balti cooking is fast, simple and delicious – and it should be fun to do. I hope you enjoy the Balti favourites in this book and, in the true spirit of Balti, feel inspired to experiment with your own ideas too.

## Cooking Equipment

The Balti pan, or karahi, is the traditional cooking vessel for Balti dishes. Originally made of cast iron, it is now available from Asian stores in a variety of metals; they are all sturdy, and therefore capable of withstanding the high cooking temperatures and sizzling oils. They are usually round-bottomed and have two circular carrying handles. Wooden stands are available, too, so the pans can be brought to the table to serve. They come in various sizes, including small ones for serving individual portions.

Balti pans are practical and add to the fun of cooking the Balti way, but they are not indispensable. A fairly thick Chinese wok or deep, round-bottomed frying pan (skillet) are good substitutes – indeed, the latter was used to produce many of the recipes in this book. Balti pans can be used for every type of Pakistan/Indian pan cooking, but they are especially suited to the quick, stir-fry cooking method used here. The other specialist cooking vessel used in the Pakistan/Indian kitchen is a tava, a flat cast-iron frying pan used for cooking parathas and other breads and for roasting spices, and again any sturdy frying pan can be substituted.

A food processor or blender is a great labour-saving tool and will be invaluable for making pastes or puréeing ingredients. Whole spices can be freshly ground the traditional way using a mortar and pestle, or, if you have one, a coffee grinder takes the chore out of the job.

You will probably find that your own kitchen is well equipped with everything else you need to produce the dishes in this book. Good-quality saucepans with heavy bases, and wooden spoons and a slotted spoon to use with them, mixing bowls, sharp knives, a chopping board, a sieve (strainer) and a rolling pin will complete the basic essentials.

## Choosing Ingredients

Good food, whatever the cuisine, depends on the quality of the ingredients used – as well as the skill of the cook. In Pakistan and India a wonderful array of fresh vegetables, fruit, herbs and spices, as well as dried spices, can be found in the numerous markets and street stalls, and a choice of the best available is often purchased on a daily basis. Nowadays, a good range of fruit, herbs and vegetables, including exotic items, can now be found in the larger supermarkets and stores in the West or can be purchased from specialist Asian stores. Baby vegetables, available from supermarkets, are especially attractive and they are used in several of the Balti

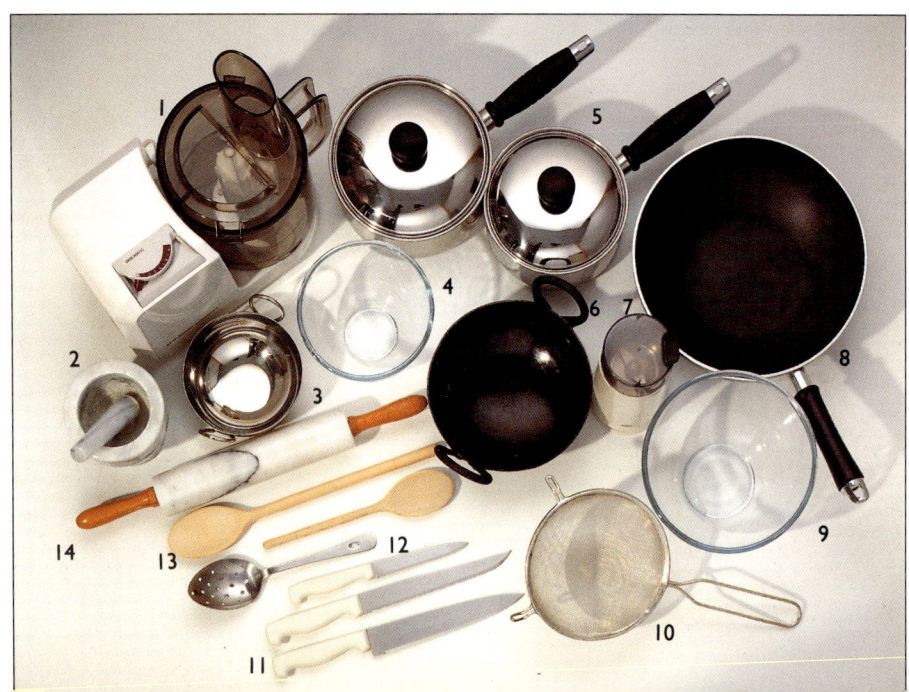

## Balti Equipment

**1** *food processor* **2** *mortar and pestle* **3** *Balti pan, or karahi, for serving individual portions* **4** *medium mixing bowl* **5** *good quality, heavy-based saucepans in two sizes* **6** *well-seasoned traditional Balti pan, or karahi* **7** *coffee grinder* **8** *deep, round-bottomed frying pan (skillet)* **9** *large mixing bowl* **10** *sieve (strainer)* **11** *sharp knives in three sizes* **12** *slotted spoon* **13** *wooden spoons* **14** *rolling pin*

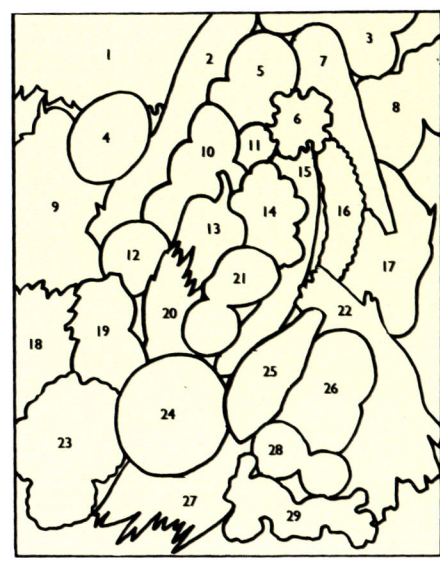

### Fresh Produce

*Fresh vegetables, herbs, fruit and spices are a must in Balti cooking. This is just a selection of those used in the recipes and includes some of the exotic-looking vegetables you might see in Asian stores.*

**1** *fresh fenugreek* **2** *mooli (white radish)* **3** *tomatoes* **4** *ripe mango* **5** *onion* **6** *fresh mint* **7** *kaddoo or doodi, which is similar to pumpkin* **8** *green (bell) pepper* **9** *fresh green chillies* **10** *green or raw (unripe) mango* **11** *garlic* **12** *red onion* **13** *red (bell) pepper* **14** *cherry tomatoes* **15** *thurai – a courgette-like Indian vegetable* **16** *karela (bitter gourd)* **17** *small aubergines (eggplants)* **18** *fresh coriander (cilantro)* **19** *pomegranate* **20** *French (green) beans* **21** *lemons* **22** *spring onions (scallions)* **23** *cauliflower florets (flowerets)* **24** *okra* **25** *sweet potato* **26** *mushrooms* **27** *baby carrots* **28** *limes* **29** *ginger*

### Home-Made Garam Masala

Garam masala can be purchased ready-ground in various mixtures. For an ultra-fresh, home-made variety, try this combination of spices.

*4 × 2.5 cm/1 in cinnamon sticks*
*3 cloves*
*3 black peppercorns*
*2 black cardamom pods, with husks removed*
*2 tsp black cumin seeds*

Grind the spices together in a coffee grinder or using a mortar and pestle until quite fine and use in any recipe calling for garam masala.

recipes here. Take advantage of the fresh produce available to produce these delicious Balti dishes, and don't be afraid to adapt the recipes, substituting other fresh vegetables if a specified ingredient can't be found on the day. Meat and poultry purchased from a good butcher is best, and if you are a regular customer they will usually pre-prepare the cuts you want, trimming, skinning and boning the meat as necessary. Fresh seafood and fish is always preferable to frozen; however, frozen foods are undoubtedly a boon for the busy cook and for quick weekday meals.

The more common spices can be found in supermarkets, and the others can be purchased from Asian stores. Some spices are available ready-ground and they keep well if stored in airtight containers. In Pakistan and India we almost always buy whole spices and grind them ourselves just prior to cooking: for a special meal the flavour can't be beaten and if you have a coffee grinder it's quite quick to do.

### A Question of Taste

The spices used in a dish are integral to its flavour and aroma. One spice can completely alter the taste of a dish and a combination of several will also effect its colour and texture. The quantities of spices and salt specified in this book are merely a guide, so feel free to experiment and increase and decrease these as you wish.

This is particularly true of chilli powder, dried red chillies and fresh green and red chillies; some brands and varieties are hotter than others. Experiment with quantities, adding less than specified, if wished. Much of the severe heat of fresh and dried chillies is contained in the seeds, and these can be removed by splitting the chillies down the middle and washing them away under cold running water. Wash your hands thoroughly with soap and water after handling cut chillies and avoid touching your face – particularly your lips and eyes – for a good while afterwards.

**Making Ginger and Garlic Pulp**

Ginger and garlic pulp is specified in many of the Balti dishes and it can be time-consuming to peel and process these everytime. It's much easier to make the pulps in large quantities and use as needed. The method is the same for both ingredients. The pulp can be stored in an airtight container or jar in the refrigerator for four to six weeks. Alternatively, freeze in ice-cube trays kept for the purpose (the pulps will taint the trays slightly). Add 1 tsp of the pulp to each compartment, freeze, remove from the tray and store in the freezer in a plastic bag.

1 Take about 225 g/8 oz ginger or garlic and soak overnight – this softens the skins and makes them easy to peel. Peel and add to a food processor or blender.

2 Process until pulped, adding a little water to get the right consistency, if necessary.

**Glossary of Special Ingredients**

**Almonds** Available whole, flaked (slivered) and ground, these sweet nuts impart a sumptuous richness to curries. They are considered a great delicacy in Pakistan and India, where they are extremely expensive.

**Bay leaves** The large dried leaves of the bay laurel tree are one of the oldest herbs used in cookery.

**Black-eyed peas** These white, kidney-shaped beans with a black 'eye' are available dried or canned.

**Cardamom pods** This spice is native to India, where it is considered to be the most prized spice after saffron. The pods can be used whole or the husks can be removed to release the seeds, and they have a slightly pungent but very aromatic taste. They come in three varieties: green, white and black. The green and white pods can be used for both sweet and savoury dishes or to flavour rice. The black pods are used only for savoury dishes.

**Chana dhal** This is a round split yellow lentil, similar in appearance to the smaller moong dhal and the larger yellow split pea, which can be used as a substitute. It is used as a binding agent in some dishes and is widely available from Asian stores.

**Chapati flour** This is a type of wholemeal (whole-wheat) flour available from Asian stores and is used to make chapatis and other breads. Ordinary wholemeal flour can be used as a substitute if well sifted.

**Chillies – dried red** These hot peppers are extremely fiery and should be used with caution. The heat can be toned down by removing the seeds before use. Dried chillies can be used whole or coarsely crushed.

**Chilli powder** Also known as cayenne pepper, this fiery ground spice should be used with caution. The heat varies from brand to brand, so adjust quantities to suit your tastebuds.

**Cinnamon** One of the earliest known spices, cinnamon has an aromatic and sweet flavour. It is sold ready-ground and as sticks, or bark.

**Cloves** This spice is used to flavour many sweet and savoury dishes and is usually added whole.

**Coriander – fresh (cilantro)** This beautifully fragrant herb is used both in cooking and sprinkled over dishes as an attractive garnish.

**Coriander seeds** This aromatic spice has a pungent, slightly lemony flavour. The seeds are used widely, either coarsely ground or in powdered form, in meat, fish and poultry dishes. Ground coriander, a brownish powder, is an important constituent of any mixture of curry spices.

**Cumin** 'White' cumin seeds are oval, ridged and greenish brown in colour. They have a strong aroma and flavour and can be used whole or ground. Ready-ground cumin powder is widely available. Black cumin seeds are dark and aromatic and are used to flavour curries and rice.

**Curry leaves** Similar in appearance to bay leaves but with a very different flavour, these can be bought dried and occasionally fresh from Asian stores.

**Fennel seeds** Very similar in appearance to cumin seeds, fennel seeds have a very sweet taste and are used to flavour certain curries. They can also be chewed as a mouth-freshener after a spicy meal.

**Fenugreek – fresh** Sold in bunches, this herb has very small leaves and is used to flavour both meat and vegetarian dishes. Always discard the stalks, which will impart a bitterness to a dish if used.

**Fenugreek seeds** These flat seeds are extremely pungent and slightly bitter.

**Garam masala** This is a mixture of spices which can be made from freshly ground spices at home or purchased ready-made. There is no set recipe, but a typical mixture might include black cumin seeds, peppercorns, cloves, cinnamon and black cardamom pods.

**Garlic** This is a standard ingredient, along with ginger, in most curries. It can be used pulped, crushed or chopped. Whole cloves are sometimes added to dishes.

**Ghee** This is clarified butter and was once the main cooking fat used in Indian/Pakistani cooking. Nowadays, vegetable ghee or vegetable oil – particularly corn oil – are used in its place, being lower in fat.

**Ginger** One of the most popular spices in India and also one of the oldest, fresh ginger is an important ingredient in many curries and is now widely available. Dried powdered ginger is a useful standby.

**Mango powder** Made from dried unripe mangoes, this has a sour taste.

**Masoor dhal** These split red lentils are actually orange in colour and turn a pale yellow when cooked. Whole brown lentils are a type of red lentil with the husk intact.

**Moong dhal** This teardrop-shaped split yellow lentil is similar to, though smaller than, chana dhal.

**Mustard seeds – black** Round in shape

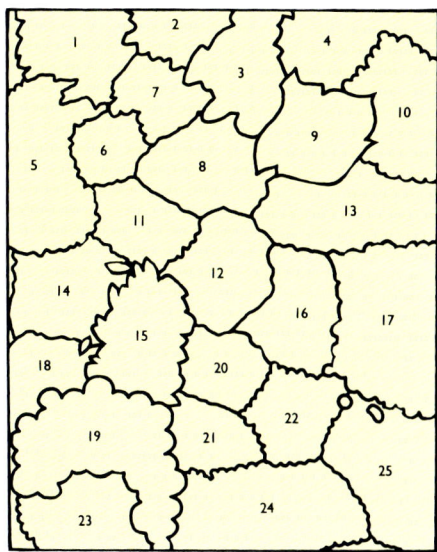

### Dried Ingredients

*These are just some of the dried spices, lentils, pulses, seeds and herbs that are used in Balti dishes:*

**1** *cinnamon bark* **2** *garam masala* **3** *black cardamom pods* **4** *onion seeds* **5** *coriander seeds* **6** *crushed dried red chillies* **7** *black peppercorns* **8** *ground cumin* **9** *bay leaves* **10** *chana dhal (split yellow lentils)* **11** *fennel seeds* **12** *ground almonds* **13** *chilli powder* **14** *black mustard seeds* **15** *green cardamom pods* **16** *urid dhal, dehulled (black gram)* **17** *black-eyed peas* **18** *fenugreek seeds* **19** *whole dried red chillies* **20** *masoor dhal, crushed (split red lentils)* **21** *urid dhal, with hull (black gram)* **22** *whole brown lentils* **23** *cardamom seeds* **24** *moong dhal (small split yellow lentils)* **25** *white sesame seeds*

and sharp in flavour, black mustard seeds are used for flavouring curries and pickles.

**Nutmeg** Although not widely used in Indian/Pakistani cooking, nutmeg is sometimes used either freshly grated or ready-ground to add an aromatic and sweet flavour.

**Onion seeds** Black in colour and triangular in shape, these seeds are widely used in pickles and to flavour vegetable curries.

**Paneer** This is a white, smooth-textured cheese, available from Asian stores. Pakistan, the home of Balti, is a meat-eating nation and cheese is not often used for cooking. However, paneer is excellent used in combination with meat and fish or as a vegetarian replacement and it appears in several of the Balti dishes in this book. (See Paneer Balti with Prawns/Shrimp for a simple recipe for home-made paneer.)

**Peppercorns** Black peppercorns are sometimes used whole with other whole spices, such as cloves, cardamom pods and bay leaves, to flavour curries. Otherwise, whenever possible, use freshly ground or crushed black pepper if the recipe calls for it.

**Pomegranate seeds** These can be extracted from fresh pomegranates or bought in jars from Asian stores and impart a delicious tangy flavour to certain curries.

**Poppy seeds** These whole seeds are usually used toasted to bring out the full flavour.

**Saffron** The world's most expensive spice is the dried stigmas of the saffron crocus, which is native to Asia Minor. To produce 450 g/2 lb of saffron requires 60,000 stigmas. Fortunately, only a small quantity of saffron is needed to flavour or colour a dish, whether sweet or savoury. Saffron is sold as strands and in powder form, and has a beautiful flavour and aroma.

**Sesame seeds** Small, whole, cream-coloured seeds, these have a slightly nutty taste and are used either plain or roasted to flavour some curries.

**Tamarind** The dried black pods of the tamarind plant are sour in taste and very sticky. Tamarind can now be bought in paste form in jars, although lemon juice can be used as a substitute.

**Toor dhal** A deep yellow, shiny split yellow lentil, toor dhal is similar in size to chana dhal.

**Turmeric** This bright yellow, bitter-tasting spice is sold ground. It is used mainly for colour rather than flavour.

**Urid dhal** This lentil is similar in size to moong dhal and is usually available split, either with the blackish hull retained or removed. Inside the lentil is a creamy white. It takes a long time to cook and has a slightly drier texture than moong dhal.

# Appetizers

*The dishes chosen here will lightly whet your appetite. The portions have been kept deliberately small, as most Balti meals include several meat, poultry or fish dishes, plus vegetable choices, as well as rice or bread. These recipes can also, of course, be served as part of a main course menu, either as accompaniments or, in larger quantities, as main courses.*

# Prawns (Shrimp) with Pomegranate Seeds

*King prawns (jumbo shrimp) are best for this dish. It makes an impressive appetizer, and is delicious served with a mixed salad.*

**SERVES 4**

INGREDIENTS

*1 tsp crushed garlic*
*1 tsp grated ginger*
*1 tsp coarsely ground pomegranate seeds*
*1 tsp ground coriander*
*1 tsp salt*
*1 tsp chilli powder*
*2 tbsp tomato purée (paste)*
*4 tbsp water*
*3 tbsp chopped fresh coriander (cilantro)*
*2 tbsp corn oil*
*12 large cooked prawns (shrimp)*
*1 medium onion, sliced into rings*

1 Put the garlic, ginger, pomegranate seeds, ground coriander, salt, chilli powder, tomato purée (paste), water and 2 tbsp of the fresh coriander (cilantro) into a bowl. Pour in the oil and blend everything together thoroughly.

2 ▲ Peel and wash the prawns and rinse them gently under running water. Using a sharp knife, make a small slit at the back of each prawn. Open out each prawn to make a butterfly shape.

3 Add the prawns to the spice mixture, making sure they are all well coated. Leave to marinate for about 2 hours.

4 ▲ Meanwhile, cut four squares of foil, about 20 × 20 cm/8 × 8 in. Preheat the oven to 230°C/450°F/Gas 8. When the prawns are ready, place 3 prawns and a few onion rings onto each square of foil, garnishing each with a little fresh coriander, and fold up into little packages. Bake for about 12–15 minutes and open up the foil to serve.

# Grilled (Broiled) Prawns (Shrimp)

*Prawns (shrimp) are delicious grilled (broiled), especially when they are flavoured with spices. Buy the largest prawns you can find for this dish.*

**SERVES 4–6**

INGREDIENTS

*18 large cooked prawns (shrimp)*
*4 tbsp lemon juice*
*1 tsp salt*
*1 tsp chilli powder*
*1 tsp garlic pulp*
*1½ tsp soft light brown sugar*
*3 tbsp corn oil*
*2 tbsp chopped fresh coriander (cilantro)*
*1 fresh green chilli, sliced*
*1 tomato, sliced*
*1 small onion, cut into rings*
*lemon wedges*

1 ▲ Peel the prawns (shrimp) and rinse them gently under cold water. Using a sharp knife, make a slit at the back of each prawn and open out into a butterfly shape. Put the remaining ingredients, with the exception of the chilli, tomato, onion and lemon wedges, in a bowl and mix together thoroughly.

2 Add the prawns to the spice mixture, making sure they are well coated, and leave to marinate for about 1 hour.

3 Place the green chilli, tomato slices and onion rings in a flameproof dish. Add the prawn mixture and cook under a very hot preheated grill (broiler) for about 10–15 minutes, basting several times with a brush. Serve immediately, garnished with the lemon wedges.

*A mixed salad of cucumber, watercress, sweetcorn (corn kernels) and cherry tomatoes, garnished with lemon wedges and onion rings (top) is delicious served with Prawns (Shrimp) with Pomegranate Seeds (centre) and Grilled (Broiled) Prawns (Shrimp).*

# Spicy Chicken and Mushroom Soup

*This creamy chicken soup makes a hearty meal for a winter's night. Serve it piping hot with fresh garlic bread.*

**SERVES 4**

**INGREDIENTS**
*225 g/8 oz chicken, skinned and boned*
*75 g/3 oz/6 tbsp unsalted butter*
*¹/2 tsp garlic pulp*
*1 tsp garam masala*
*1 tsp crushed black peppercorns*
*1 tsp salt*
*¹/4 tsp ground nutmeg*
*1 medium leek, sliced*
*75 g/3 oz/1 cup mushrooms, sliced*
*50 g/2 oz/¹/3 cup sweetcorn (corn kernels)*
*300 ml/¹/2 pint/1¹/4 cups water*
*250 ml/8 fl oz/1 cup single (light) cream*
*1 tbsp chopped fresh coriander (cilantro)*
*1 tsp crushed dried red chillies (optional)*

1 Cut the chicken pieces into very fine strips.

2 ▲ Melt the butter in a medium saucepan. Lower the heat slightly and add the garlic and garam masala. Lower the heat even further and add the black peppercorns, salt and nutmeg. Finally, add the chicken pieces, leek, mushrooms and sweetcorn (corn kernels), and cook for 5–7 minutes or until the chicken is cooked through, stirring constantly.

3 ▲ Remove from the heat and allow to cool slightly. Transfer three-quarters of the mixture into a food processor or blender. Add the water and process for about 1 minute.

4 Pour the resulting purée back into the saucepan with the rest of the mixture and bring to the boil over a medium heat. Lower the heat and stir in the cream.

5 ▲ Add the fresh coriander (cilantro) and taste for seasoning. Serve hot, garnished with the crushed red chillies, if wished.

# Chicken and Almond Soup

*This soup makes an excellent appetizer and served with Naan will also make a satisfying lunch or supper dish.*

**SERVES 4**

INGREDIENTS
75 g/3 oz/6 tbsp unsalted butter
1 medium leek, chopped
½ tsp shredded ginger
75 g/3 oz/1 cup ground almonds
1 tsp salt
½ tsp crushed black peppercorns
1 fresh green chilli, chopped
1 medium carrot, sliced
50 g/2 oz/½ cup frozen peas
115g/4 oz/¾ cup chicken, skinned, boned
    and cubed
1 tbsp chopped fresh coriander (cilantro)
450 ml/¾ pint/scant 2 cups water
250 ml/8 fl oz/1 cup single (light) cream
4 coriander sprigs

1   Melt the butter in a large karahi or deep round-bottomed frying pan (skillet), and sauté the leek with the ginger until soft.

2 ▲ Lower the heat and add the ground almonds, salt, peppercorns, chilli, carrot, peas and chicken. Fry for about 10 minutes or until the chicken is completely cooked, stirring constantly. Add the chopped fresh coriander (cilantro).

3 ▲ Remove from the heat and allow to cool slightly. Transfer the mixture to a food processor or blender and process for about 1½ minutes. Pour in the water and blend for a further 30 seconds.

4 ▲ Pour back into the saucepan and bring to the boil, stirring occasionally. Once it has boiled, lower the heat and gradually stir in the cream. Cook gently for a further 2 minutes, stirring occasionally.

5   Serve garnished with the fresh coriander sprigs.

# Chicken Kofta Balti with Paneer

*This rather unusual appetizer looks most elegant when served in small individual karahis.*

**SERVES 6**

INGREDIENTS
**Koftas**
450 g/1 lb/3¼ cups chicken, skinned,
    boned and cubed
1 tsp garlic pulp
1 tsp shredded ginger
1½ tsp ground coriander
1½ tsp chilli powder
½ tsp ground fenugreek
¼ tsp turmeric
1 tsp salt
2 tbsp chopped fresh coriander (cilantro)
2 fresh green chillies, chopped
600 ml/1 pint/2½ cups water
corn oil for frying

**Paneer mixture**
1 medium onion, sliced
1 red (bell) pepper, seeded and cut
    into strips
1 green (bell) pepper, seeded and cut
    into strips
175 g/6 oz paneer, cubed
175 g/6 oz/1 cup sweetcorn (corn kernels)

mint sprigs
1 dried red chilli, crushed (optional)

1 ▲ Put all the kofta ingredients, apart from the oil, into a medium saucepan. Bring to the boil slowly, over a medium heat, and cook until all the liquid has evaporated.

2 ▲ Remove from the heat and allow to cool slightly. Put the mixture into a food processor or blender and process for 2 minutes, stopping once or twice to loosen the mixture with a spoon.

3 ▲ Scrape the mixture into a large mixing bowl using a wooden spoon. Taking a little of the mixture at a time, shape it into small balls using your hands. You should be able to make about 12 koftas.

4 ▲ Heat the oil in a karahi or deep round-bottomed frying pan (skillet) over a high heat. Turn the heat down slightly and drop the koftas carefully into the oil. Move them around gently to ensure that they cook evenly.

5 When the koftas are lightly browned, remove them from the oil with a slotted spoon and drain on kitchen paper (paper towels). Set to one side.

6 ▲ Heat up the oil still remaining in the karahi, and flash fry all the ingredients for the paneer mixture. This should take about 3 minutes over a high heat.

7 ▲ Divide the paneer mixture evenly between 6 individual karahis. Add 2 koftas to each serving, and garnish with mint sprigs and the crushed red chilli, if wished.

# Chicken and Pasta Balti

*This is not a traditional Balti dish, as pasta is not eaten widely in India or Pakistan, however, I have included it here as it is truly delicious! The pomegranate seeds give this dish an unusual tangy flavour.*

**SERVES 4–6**

### INGREDIENTS

75 g/3 oz/³/4 cup small pasta shells (the coloured ones look most attractive)
5 tbsp corn oil
4 curry leaves
4 whole dried red chillies
1 large onion, sliced
1 tsp garlic pulp
1 tsp chilli powder
1 tsp shredded ginger
1 tsp crushed pomegranate seeds
1 tsp salt
2 medium tomatoes, chopped
175 g/6 oz/1¹/3 cups chicken, skinned, boned and cubed
225 g/8 oz/1¹/2 cups canned chick-peas (garbanzos), drained

115 g/4 oz/²/3 cup sweetcorn (corn kernels)
50 g/2 oz mange-tout (snow peas), diagonally sliced
1 tbsp chopped fresh coriander (cilantro) (optional)

1 ▲ Cook the pasta in boiling water, following the directions on the package. Add 1 tbsp of the oil to the water to prevent the pasta from sticking together. When it is cooked, drain and set to one side in a sieve (strainer).

2 ▲ Heat the remaining oil in a deep round-bottomed frying pan (skillet) or a large karahi, and add the curry leaves, whole dried chillies and the onion. Fry for about 5 minutes.

3  Add the garlic, chilli powder, ginger, pomegranate seeds, salt and tomatoes. Stir-fry for about 3 minutes.

4 ▲ Next add the chicken, chick-peas (garbanzos), sweetcorn (corn kernels) and mange-tout (snow peas) to the onion mixture. Cook over a medium heat for about 5 minutes, stirring.

5 ▲ Tip in the pasta and stir well. Cook for a further 7–10 minutes until the chicken is cooked through.

6  Serve garnished with the fresh coriander (cilantro) if wished.

# Balti Lamb Chops with Potatoes

*These chops are marinated before being cooked in a delicious spicy sauce. They make a good appetizer, served with a simple mixed salad.*

**SERVES 6–8**

### INGREDIENTS

*8 lamb chops (about 50–75 g/2–3 oz each)*
*2 tbsp olive oil*
*150 ml/¼ pint/⅔ cup lemon juice*
*1 tsp salt*
*1 tbsp chopped fresh mint and coriander (cilantro)*
*150 ml/¼ pint/⅔ cup corn oil*
*mint sprigs*
*lime slices*

### Sauce

*3 tbsp corn oil*
*8 medium tomatoes, roughly chopped*
*1 bay leaf*
*1 tsp garam masala*
*2 tbsp natural (plain) yogurt*
*1 tsp garlic pulp*
*1 tsp chilli powder*
*1 tsp salt*
*½ tsp black cumin seeds*
*3 black peppercorns*
*2 medium potatoes, peeled, roughly chopped and boiled*

**1 ▲** Put the chops into a large bowl. Mix together the olive oil, lemon juice, salt and fresh mint and coriander (cilantro). Pour the oil mixture over the chops and rub it in well with your fingers. Leave to marinate for at least 3 hours.

**2 ▲** To make the sauce, heat the corn oil in a deep round-bottomed frying pan (skillet) or a karahi. Lower the heat and add the chopped tomatoes. Stir-fry for about 2 minutes. Gradually add the bay leaf, garam masala, yogurt, garlic, chilli powder, salt, black cumin seeds and peppercorns, and stir-fry for a further 2–3 minutes.

**3** Lower the heat again and add the cooked potatoes, mixing everything together well. Remove from the heat and set to one side.

**4 ▲** Heat 150 ml/¼ pint/⅔ cup corn oil in a separate frying pan. Lower the heat slightly and fry the marinated chops until they are cooked through. This will take about 10–12 minutes. Remove with a slotted spoon and drain the cooked chops on kitchen paper (paper towels).

**5** Heat the sauce in the karahi, bringing it to the boil. Add the chops and lower the heat. Simmer for 5–7 minutes.

**6** Transfer to a warmed serving dish and garnish with the mint sprigs and lime slices.

# Chicken Dishes

*Chicken is one of the more expensive meats on the Indian sub-continent and highly favoured – a chicken dish cooked in one form or another is a must at Pakistani weddings. Chicken is also very versatile and can be beautifully cooked dry, in a sauce, or with vegetables. It also cooks much more quickly than other meats and is therefore especially suited to Balti. Balti Chicken is the most popular of all Balti dishes, but many others in this chapter are equally renowned and just as delicious.*

# Balti Chicken

*This recipe has a beautifully delicate flavour, and is probably the most popular of all Balti dishes. Choose a young chicken as it will be more flavoursome.*

**SERVES 4–6**

**INGREDIENTS**

1–1½ kg/2½–3 lb chicken, skinned and
   cut into 8 pieces
3 tbsp corn oil
3 medium onions, sliced
3 medium tomatoes, halved and sliced
2.5 cm/1 in cinnamon stick
2 large black cardamom pods
4 black peppercorns
½ tsp black cumin seeds
1 tsp ginger pulp
1 tsp garlic pulp
1 tsp garam masala
1 tsp chilli powder
1 tsp salt
2 tbsp natural (plain) yogurt
4 tbsp lemon juice
2 tbsp chopped fresh coriander (cilantro)
2 fresh green chillies, chopped

1  Wash and trim the chicken pieces, and set to one side.

**2 ▲** Heat the oil in a large karahi or deep round-bottomed frying pan (skillet). Throw in the onions and fry until they are golden brown. Add the tomatoes and stir well.

**3 ▲** Add the cinnamon stick, cardamoms, peppercorns, black cumin seeds, ginger, garlic, garam masala, chilli powder and salt. Lower the heat and stir-fry for 3–5 minutes.

**4 ▲** Add the chicken pieces, 2 at a time, and stir-fry for at least 7 minutes or until the spice mixture has completely penetrated the chicken pieces.

**5 ▲** Add the yogurt to the chicken and mix well.

**6**  Lower the heat and cover the pan with a piece of foil, making sure that the foil does not touch the food. Cook very gently for about 15 minutes, checking once to make sure the food is not catching on the bottom of the pan.

**7 ▲** Finally, add the lemon juice, fresh coriander (cilantro) and green chillies, and serve at once.

**COOK'S TIP**

*Chicken cooked on the bone is both tender and flavoursome. However, do substitute the whole chicken with 675 g/1½ lb boned and cubed chicken, if wished. The cooking time can be reduced at step 6, too.*

# Balti Chicken in Saffron Sauce

*This is a beautifully aromatic chicken dish that is partly cooked in the oven. It contains saffron, the most expensive spice in the world, and is sure to impress your guests.*

**SERVES 4–6**

INGREDIENTS
50 g/2 oz/4 tbsp butter
2 tbsp corn oil
1–1½ kg/2½–3 lb chicken, skinned and
    cut into 8 pieces
1 medium onion, chopped
1 tsp garlic pulp
½ tsp crushed black peppercorns
½ tsp crushed cardamom pods
¼ tsp ground cinnamon
1½ tsp chilli powder
150 ml/¼ pint/⅔ cup natural (plain)
    yogurt
50 g/2 oz/½ cup ground almonds
1 tbsp lemon juice
1 tsp salt
1 tsp saffron strands
150 ml/¼ pint/⅔ cup water
150 ml/¼ pint/⅔ cup single (light) cream
2 tbsp chopped fresh coriander (cilantro)

I ▲ Preheat the oven to 180°C/350°F/ Gas 4. Melt the butter with the oil in a deep round-bottomed frying pan (skillet) or a medium karahi. Add the chicken pieces and fry until lightly browned. This will take about 5 minutes. Remove the chicken using a slotted spoon, leaving behind as much of the fat as possible.

2 ▲ Add the onion to the same pan, and fry over a medium heat. Meanwhile, mix together the garlic, black peppercorns, cardamom, cinnamon, chilli powder, yogurt, ground almonds, lemon juice, salt and saffron strands in a mixing bowl.

3 ▲ When the onions are lightly browned, pour the spice mixture into the pan and stir-fry for about 1 minute.

4 ▲ Add the chicken pieces, and continue to stir-fry for a further 2 minutes. Add the water and bring to a simmer.

5  Transfer the contents of the pan to a casserole dish and cover with a lid, or, if using a karahi, cover with foil. Transfer to the oven and cook for 30–35 minutes.

6 ▲ Once you are sure that the chicken is cooked right through, remove it from the oven. Transfer the chicken to a frying pan and stir in the cream.

7  Reheat gently on the hob for about 2 minutes. Garnish with fresh coriander (cilantro) and serve with Fruity Pullao or plain boiled rice.

**COOK'S TIP**

*There is no substitute for saffron, so don't be tempted to use turmeric instead. It is well worth buying a small amount of saffron – either strands or in powdered form – to create this dish for a special occasion.*

# Balti Chicken with Vegetables

*In this recipe the chicken and vegetables are cut into strips which makes the dish particularly attractive.*

**SERVES 4–6**

INGREDIENTS

4 tbsp corn oil
2 medium onions, sliced
4 garlic cloves, thickly sliced
450 g/1 lb/3¼ cups chicken breast, skinned, boned and cut into strips
1 tsp salt
2 tbsp lime juice
3 fresh green chillies, chopped
2 medium carrots, cut into batons
2 medium potatoes, peeled and cut into 1 cm/½ in strips
1 medium courgette (zucchini), cut into batons
4 lime slices
1 tbsp chopped fresh coriander (cilantro)
2 fresh green chillies, cut into strips (optional)

1  Heat the oil in a large karahi or deep round-bottomed frying pan (skillet). Lower the heat slightly and add the onions. Fry until lightly browned.

2 ▲ Add half the garlic slices and fry for a few seconds before adding the chicken and salt. Cook everything together, stirring, until all the moisture has evaporated and the chicken is lightly browned.

3 ▲ Add the lime juice, green chillies and all the vegetables to the pan. Turn up the heat and add the rest of the garlic. Stir-fry for 7–10 minutes, or until the chicken is cooked through and the vegetables are just tender.

4  Transfer to a serving dish and garnish with the lime slices, fresh coriander (cilantro) and green chilli strips, if wished.

# Balti Chilli Chicken

*Hot and spicy would be the best way of describing this mouth-watering Balti dish. The smell of the fresh chillies cooking is indescribable!*

**SERVES 4–6**

INGREDIENTS

5 tbsp corn oil
8 large fresh green chillies, slit
½ tsp mixed onion and cumin seeds
4 curry leaves
1 tsp ginger pulp
1 tsp chilli powder
1 tsp ground coriander
1 tsp garlic pulp
1 tsp salt
2 medium onions, chopped
675 g/1½ lb/4⅔ cups chicken, skinned, boned and cubed
1 tbsp lemon juice
1 tbsp roughly chopped fresh mint
1 tbsp roughly chopped fresh coriander (cilantro)
8–10 cherry tomatoes

**2 ▲** Add the onion and cumin seeds, curry leaves, ginger, chilli powder, ground coriander, garlic, salt and onions, and fry for a few seconds, stirring continuously.

**3** Add the chicken pieces and stir-fry for 7–10 minutes, or until the chicken is cooked right through.

**4 ▼** Sprinkle on the lemon juice and add the mint and coriander (cilantro).

**5** Add the cherry tomatoes and serve with Naan or Paratha.

**I ▲** Heat the oil in a deep round-bottomed frying pan (skillet) or a medium karahi. Lower the heat slightly and add the slit green chillies. Fry until the skin starts to change colour.

# Balti Butter Chicken

*Butter Chicken is one of the most popular Balti chicken dishes, especially in the West. Cooked in butter, with aromatic spices, cream and almonds, this mild dish will be enjoyed by everyone. Serve with Colourful Pullao Rice.*

**SERVES 4–6**

INGREDIENTS

150 ml/¼ pint/⅔ cup natural (plain) yogurt
50 g/2 oz/½ cup ground almonds
1½ tsp chilli powder
¼ tsp crushed bay leaves
¼ tsp ground cloves
¼ tsp ground cinnamon
1 tsp garam masala
4 green cardamom pods
1 tsp ginger pulp
1 tsp garlic pulp
400 g/14 oz/2 cups canned tomatoes
1¼ tsp salt
1 kg/2 lb/6½ cups chicken, skinned, boned and cubed
75 g/3 oz/6 tbsp butter
1 tbsp corn oil
2 medium onions, sliced
2 tbsp chopped fresh coriander (cilantro)
4 tbsp single (light) cream
coriander sprigs

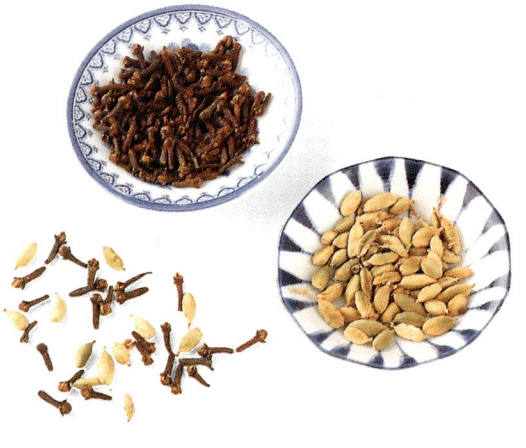

1 ▲ Put the yogurt, ground almonds, all the dry spices, ginger, garlic, tomatoes and salt into a mixing bowl and blend together thoroughly.

2 ▲ Put the chicken into a large mixing bowl and pour over the yogurt mixture. Set aside.

3  Melt together the butter and oil in a medium karahi or deep round-bottomed frying pan (skillet). Add the onions and fry for about 3 minutes.

4 ▲ Add the chicken mixture and stir-fry for 7–10 minutes.

5 ▲ Stir in about half of the coriander (cilantro) and mix well.

6 ▲ Pour over the cream and stir in well. Bring to the boil. Serve garnished with the remaining chopped coriander and coriander sprigs.

**COOK'S TIP**

*Substitute natural (plain) yogurt with Greek-style yogurt for an even richer and creamier flavour.*

# Balti Chicken with Lentils

*This is rather an unusual combination of flavours, but I do recommend you try it. The mango powder gives a delicious tangy flavour to this spicy dish.*

**SERVES 4–6**

INGREDIENTS
75 g/3 oz/½ cup chana dhal (split yellow
    lentils)
4 tbsp corn oil
2 medium leeks, chopped
6 large dried red chillies
4 curry leaves
1 tsp mustard seeds
2 tsp mango powder
2 medium tomatoes, chopped
½ tsp chilli powder
1 tsp ground coriander
1 tsp salt
450 g/1 lb/3¼ cups chicken, skinned,
    boned and cubed
1 tbsp chopped fresh coriander (cilantro)

1  Wash the lentils carefully and remove any stones.

2 ▲ Put the lentils into a saucepan with enough water to cover, and boil for about 10 minutes until they are soft but not mushy. Drain and set to one side in a bowl.

3 ▲ Heat the oil in a medium karahi or deep round-bottomed frying pan (skillet). Lower the heat slightly and throw in the leeks, dried red chillies, curry leaves and mustard seeds. Stir-fry gently for a few minutes.

4 ▲ Add the mango powder, tomatoes, chilli powder, ground coriander, salt and chicken, and stir-fry for 7–10 minutes.

5 ▲ Mix in the cooked lentils and fry for a further 2 minutes, or until you are sure that the chicken is cooked right through.

6  Garnish with fresh coriander (cilantro) and serve with Paratha.

**COOK'S TIP**

*Chana dhal, a split yellow lentil, is available from Asian stores. However, split yellow peas are a good substitute.*

# Balti Baby Chicken in Tamarind Sauce

*The tamarind in this recipe gives the dish a sweet-and-sour flavour; this is also quite a hot Balti.*

## SERVES 4–6

### INGREDIENTS

4 tbsp tomato ketchup
1 tbsp tamarind paste
4 tbsp water
1½ tsp chilli powder
1½ tsp salt
1 tbsp sugar
1½ tsp ginger pulp
1½ tsp garlic pulp
2 tbsp desiccated (shredded) coconut
2 tbsp sesame seeds
1 tsp poppy seeds
1 tsp ground cumin
1½ tsp ground coriander
2 × 450 g/1 lb baby chickens, skinned and
    cut into 6–8 pieces each
5 tbsp corn oil
8 tbsp curry leaves
½ tsp onion seeds
3 large dried red chillies
½ tsp fenugreek seeds
10–12 cherry tomatoes
3 tbsp chopped fresh coriander (cilantro)
2 fresh green chillies, chopped

I ▲ Put the tomato ketchup, tamarind paste and water into a large mixing bowl and use a fork to blend everything together.

2 ▲ Add the chilli powder, salt, sugar, ginger, garlic, coconut, sesame and poppy seeds, ground cumin and ground coriander to the mixture.

3 ▲ Add the chicken pieces and stir until they are well coated with the spice mixture. Set to one side.

4 ▲ Heat the oil in a deep round-bottomed frying pan (skillet) or a large karahi. Add the curry leaves, onion seeds, dried red chillies and fenugreek seeds and fry for about 1 minute.

5 ▲ Lower the heat to medium and add the chicken pieces, along with their sauce, 2 or 3 pieces at a time, mixing as you go. When all the pieces are in the pan, stir them around well using a slotted spoon.

6 Simmer gently for about 12–15 minutes, or until the chicken is thoroughly cooked.

7 ▲ Finally, add the tomatoes, fresh coriander (cilantro) and green chillies, and serve with Fried Rice with Cashew Nuts, if wished.

# Sweet-and-Sour Balti Chicken

*This dish combines a sweet-and-sour flavour with a creamy texture. It is delicious served with Colourful Pullao Rice or Naan.*

**SERVES 4**

INGREDIENTS

*3 tbsp tomato purée (paste)*
*2 tbsp Greek-style yogurt*
*1½ tsp garam masala*
*1 tsp chilli powder*
*1 tsp garlic pulp*
*2 tbsp mango chutney*
*1 tsp salt*
*½ tsp sugar (optional)*
*4 tbsp corn oil*
*675 g/1½ lb/4⅔ cups chicken, skinned, boned and cubed*
*150 ml/¼ pint/⅔ cup water*
*2 fresh green chillies, chopped*
*2 tbsp chopped fresh coriander (cilantro)*
*2 tbsp single (light) cream*

1 ▲ Blend together the tomato purée (paste), yogurt, garam masala, chilli powder, garlic, mango chutney, salt and sugar (if using) in a medium mixing bowl.

2 ▲ Heat the oil in a deep round-bottomed frying pan (skillet) or a large karahi. Lower the heat slightly and pour in the spice mixture. Bring to the boil and cook for about 2 minutes, stirring occasionally.

3 ▲ Add the chicken pieces and stir until they are well coated.

4 Add the water to thin the sauce slightly. Continue cooking for 5–7 minutes, or until the chicken is tender.

5 ▲ Finally add the fresh chillies, coriander (cilantro) and cream, and cook for a further 2 minutes until the chicken is cooked through.

# Balti Chicken Pasanda

*P*asanda dishes are firm favourites in
Pakistan, but they are also becoming
well known in the West.

**SERVES 4**

INGREDIENTS

4 tbsp Greek-style yogurt
½ tsp black cumin seeds
4 cardamom pods
6 whole black peppercorns
2 tsp garam masala
2.5 cm/1 in cinnamon stick
1 tbsp ground almonds
1 tsp garlic pulp
1 tsp ginger pulp
1 tsp chilli powder
1 tsp salt
675 g/1½ lb/4⅔ cups chicken, skinned,
   boned and cubed
5 tbsp corn oil
2 medium onions, diced
3 fresh green chillies, chopped
2 tbsp chopped fresh coriander (cilantro)
120 ml/4 fl oz/½ cup single (light) cream

**3 ▲** Pour in the chicken mixture and
stir until it is well blended with the
onions.

**4 ▲** Cook over a medium heat for 12–
15 minutes or until the sauce thickens
and the chicken is cooked through.

**5 ▲** Add the green chillies and fresh
coriander (cilantro), and pour in the
cream. Bring to the boil and serve
garnished with more coriander, if
wished.

**COOK'S TIP**

This Balti dish has a lovely thick sauce
and is especially good served with one of
the rice dishes from this book.

**I ▲** Mix the yogurt, cumin seeds,
cardamoms, peppercorns, garam
masala, cinnamon stick, ground
almonds, garlic, ginger, chilli powder
and salt in a medium mixing bowl. Add
the chicken pieces and leave to
marinate for about 2 hours.

**2** Heat the oil in a large karahi or deep
round-bottomed frying pan (skillet).
Throw in the onions and fry for 2–3
minutes.

# Chicken and Tomato Balti

*If you like tomatoes, you will love this chicken recipe. It makes a semi-dry Balti and is good served with a lentil dish and plain boiled rice.*

## SERVES 4

INGREDIENTS
*4 tbsp corn oil*
*6 curry leaves*
*1/2 tsp mixed onion and mustard seeds*
*8 medium tomatoes, sliced*
*1 tsp ground coriander*
*1 tsp chilli powder*
*1 tsp salt*
*1 tsp ground cumin*
*1 tsp garlic pulp*
*675 g/1 1/2 lb/4 2/3 cups chicken, skinned, boned and cubed*
*150 ml/1/4 pint/2/3 cup water*
*1 tbsp sesame seeds, roasted*
*1 tbsp chopped fresh coriander (cilantro)*

I ▲ Heat the oil in a deep round-bottomed frying pan (skillet) or a medium karahi. Add the curry leaves and mixed onion and mustard seeds and stir well.

2 ▲ Lower the heat slightly and add the tomatoes.

3 ▲ While the tomatoes are gently cooking, mix together the ground coriander, chilli powder, salt, ground cumin and garlic in a bowl. Tip the spices onto the tomatoes.

4 ▲ Add the chicken pieces and stir together well. Stir-fry for about 5 minutes.

5  Pour on the water and continue cooking, stirring occasionally, until the sauce thickens and the chicken is cooked through.

6 ▲ Sprinkle the sesame seeds and fresh coriander (cilantro) over the top of the dish and serve.

## COOK'S TIP

*Sesame seeds are available from Asian and health food stores. There are two types – unroasted seeds, which are white, and roasted ones, which are lightly browned. To roast sesame seeds at home, simply tip a quantity into a frying pan (skillet) over a high heat for about 1 minute. Shake the pan constantly to prevent the seeds burning. Use immediately or store in a screw-topped jar.*

# Khara Masala Balti Chicken

*Whole spices (khara) are used in this recipe, giving it a wonderfully rich flavour. This is a dry dish so it is best served with Raita and Paratha.*

**SERVES 4**

**INGREDIENTS**

*3 curry leaves*
*1/4 tsp mustard seeds*
*1/4 tsp fennel seeds*
*1/4 tsp onion seeds*
*1/2 tsp crushed dried red chillies*
*1/2 tsp white cumin seeds*
*1/4 tsp fenugreek seeds*
*1/2 tsp crushed pomegranate seeds*
*1 tsp salt*
*1 tsp shredded ginger*
*3 garlic cloves, sliced*
*4 tbsp corn oil*
*4 fresh green chillies, slit*
*1 large onion, sliced*
*1 medium tomato, sliced*
*675 g/1 1/2 lb/4 2/3 cups chicken, skinned, boned and cubed*
*1 tbsp chopped fresh coriander (cilantro)*

1 ▲ Mix together the curry leaves, mustard seeds, fennel seeds, onion seeds, crushed red chillies, cumin seeds, fenugreek seeds, crushed pomegranate seeds and salt in a large bowl.

2 ▲ Add the shredded ginger and garlic cloves.

3 ▲ Heat the oil in a medium karahi or deep round-bottomed frying pan (skillet). Add the spice mixture and throw in the green chillies.

4 ▲ Tip in the onion and stir-fry over a medium heat for 5–7 minutes.

5 ▲ Finally add the tomato and chicken pieces, and cook over a medium heat for about 7 minutes. The chicken should be cooked through and the sauce reduced.

6 ▲ Stir everything together over the heat for a further 3–5 minutes, and **serve** garnished with chopped fresh coriander (cilantro).

# Fish & Seafood Dishes

*Saltwater and freshwater fish are eaten in Pakistan, and Karachi, on the coast, is particularly known for its delicious seafood. Firm-fleshed fish and many types of seafood work particularly well in Balti dishes and offer a more healthy alternative to meat dishes. Fish and seafood dishes are also very easy to cook and make an excellent choice for quick weekday meals.*

# Balti Fried Fish

*As a child in Pakistan, I used to hear fishmongers calling out the contents of their day's catch from stalls on wheels. Nowadays, seafood is readily available in the many fish markets.*

**SERVES 4–6**

**INGREDIENTS**
675 g/1½ lb cod, or any other firm,
    white fish
1 medium onion, sliced
1 tbsp lemon juice
1 tsp salt
1 tsp garlic pulp
1 tsp crushed dried red chillies
1½ tsp garam masala
2 tbsp chopped fresh coriander (cilantro)
2 medium tomatoes
2 tbsp cornflour (cornstarch)
150 ml/¼ pint/⅔ cup corn oil

1   Skin the fish and cut into small cubes. Put into the refrigerator to chill.

2 ▲ Put the onion into a bowl and add the lemon juice, salt, garlic, crushed red chillies, garam masala and fresh coriander (cilantro). Mix together well and set to one side.

3 ▲ Skin the tomatoes by dropping them into boiling water for a few seconds. Remove with a slotted spoon and gently peel off the skins. Chop the tomatoes roughly and add to the onion mixture in the bowl.

4 ▲ Place the contents of the bowl into a food processor or blender and process for about 30 seconds.

5   Remove the fish from the refrigerator. Pour the contents of the food processor or blender over the fish and mix together well.

6 ▲ Add the cornflour (cornstarch) and mix again until the fish pieces are well coated.

7 ▲ Heat the oil in a deep round-bottomed frying pan (skillet) or a karahi. Lower the heat slightly and add the fish pieces, a few at a time. Turn them gently with a slotted spoon as they will break easily. Cook for about 5 minutes until the fish is lightly browned.

8   Remove the fish pieces from the pan and drain on kitchen paper (paper towels) to absorb any excess oil. Keep warm and continue frying the remaining fish. This dish is delicious served with Apricot Chutney and Paratha.

**COOK'S TIP**

*For busy cooks, canned tomatoes can be used instead of fresh ones – there are no skins to remove!*

# Chunky Fish Balti with Peppers

*Try to find as many different colours of (bell) peppers as possible to make this very attractive dish.*

**SERVES 2–4**

❀❀❀❀❀❀❀❀❀❀❀❀❀❀❀❀

INGREDIENTS

450 g/1 lb cod, or any other firm, white
   fish
1½ tsp ground cumin
2 tsp mango powder
1 tsp ground coriander
½ tsp chilli powder
1 tsp salt
1 tsp ginger pulp
3 tbsp cornflour (cornstarch)
150 ml/¼ pint/⅔ cup corn oil
1 each green, orange and red (bell)
   peppers, seeded and chopped
8–10 cherry tomatoes

❀❀❀❀❀❀❀❀❀❀❀❀❀❀❀❀

1 ▲ Skin the fish and cut into small cubes. Put the cubes into a large mixing bowl and add the ground cumin, mango powder, ground coriander, chilli powder, salt, ginger and cornflour (cornstarch). Mix together thoroughly until the fish is well coated.

2 ▲ Heat the oil in a deep round-bottomed frying pan (skillet) or a medium karahi. Lower the heat slightly and add the fish pieces, 3 or 4 at a time. Fry for about 3 minutes, turning constantly.

3 Drain the fish pieces on kitchen paper (paper towels) and transfer to a serving dish. Keep warm and fry the remaining fish pieces.

4 ▲ Fry the (bell) peppers in the remaining oil for about 2 minutes. They should still be slightly crisp. Drain on kitchen paper.

5 Add the cooked peppers to the fish on the serving dish and garnish with the cherry tomatoes. Serve immediately with Raita and Paratha, if wished.

# Balti Fish Fillets in Spicy Coconut Sauce

*Use fresh fish fillets to make this dish if you can, as they have much more flavour than frozen ones. However, if you are using frozen fillets, ensure that they are completely thawed before using.*

**SERVES 4**

**INGREDIENTS**
*2 tbsp corn oil*
*1 tsp onion seeds*
*4 dried red chillies*
*3 garlic cloves, sliced*
*1 medium onion, sliced*
*2 medium tomatoes, sliced*
*2 tbsp desiccated (shredded) coconut*
*1 tsp salt*
*1 tsp ground coriander*
*4 flatfish fillets, such as plaice, sole or flounder, each about 75 g/3 oz*
*150 ml/¼ pint/⅔ cup water*
*1 tbsp lime juice*
*1 tbsp chopped fresh coriander (cilantro)*

**2 ▲** Add the tomatoes, coconut, salt and coriander and stir thoroughly.

**3 ▲** Cut each fish fillet into 3 pieces. Drop the fish pieces into the mixture and turn them over gently until they are well coated.

**4** Cook for 5–7 minutes, lowering the heat if necessary. Add the water, lime juice and fresh coriander (cilantro) and cook for a further 3–5 minutes until the water has mostly evaporated. Serve immediately with rice.

**1 ▲** Heat the oil in a deep round-bottomed frying pan (skillet) or a karahi. Lower the heat slightly and add the onion seeds, dried red chillies, garlic slices and onion. Cook for 3–4 minutes, stirring once or twice.

# Balti Prawns (Shrimp) and Vegetables in Thick Sauce

*Here, tender prawns (shrimp), crunchy vegetables and a thick curry sauce combine to produce a dish rich in flavour and texture. Fruity Pullao is a perfect accompaniment, although plain rice is a good alternative.*

**SERVES 4**

INGREDIENTS

*3 tbsp corn oil*
*1 tsp mixed fenugreek, mustard and onion seeds*
*2 curry leaves*
*½ medium cauliflower, cut into small florets (flowerets)*
*8 baby carrots, halved lengthways*
*6 new potatoes, thickly sliced*
*50 g/2 oz/½ cup frozen peas*
*2 medium onions, sliced*
*2 tbsp tomato purée (paste)*
*1½ tsp chilli powder*
*1 tsp ground coriander*
*1 tsp ginger pulp*
*1 tsp garlic pulp*
*1 tsp salt*
*2 tbsp lemon juice*
*450 g/1 lb cooked prawns (shrimp)*
*2 tbsp chopped fresh coriander (cilantro)*
*1 fresh red chilli, seeded and sliced*
*120 ml/4 fl oz/½ cup single (light) cream*

I ▲ Heat the oil in a deep round-bottomed frying pan (skillet) or a large karahi. Lower the heat slightly and add the fenugreek, mustard and onion seeds and the curry leaves.

2 ▲ Turn up the heat and add the cauliflower, carrots, potatoes and peas. Stir-fry quickly until browned, then remove from the pan with a slotted spoon and drain on kitchen paper (paper towels).

3  Add the onions to the oil left in the karahi and fry over a medium heat until golden brown.

4 ▲ While the onions are cooking, mix together the tomato purée (paste), chilli powder, ground coriander, ginger, garlic, salt and lemon juice and pour the paste onto the onions.

5  Add the prawns (shrimp) and stir-fry over a low heat for about 5 minutes or until they are heated through.

6 ▲ Add the fried vegetables to the pan and mix together well.

7 ▲ Add the fresh coriander (cilantro) and red chilli and pour over the cream. Bring to the boil and serve immediately.

**VARIATION**

*Monkfish is an excellent alternative to the prawns (shrimp) used in this recipe, as it is a firm-fleshed fish that will not break up when fried. Cut the monkfish into chunks, add to the onion and spice mixture at step 5 and stir-fry over a low heat for 5–7 minutes or until the fish is cooked through.*

# Paneer Balti with Prawns (Shrimp)

*Although paneer is not widely eaten in Pakistan, it makes an excellent substitute for red meat. Here it is combined with king prawns (jumbo shrimp) to make one of my favourite dishes.*

**SERVES 4**

INGREDIENTS

12 cooked king prawns (jumbo shrimp)
175 g/6 oz paneer
2 tbsp tomato purée (paste)
4 tbsp Greek-style yogurt
1½ tsp garam masala
1 tsp chilli powder
1 tsp garlic pulp
1 tsp salt
2 tsp mango powder
1 tsp ground coriander
115 g/4 oz/8 tbsp butter
1 tbsp corn oil
3 fresh green chillies, chopped
3 tbsp chopped fresh coriander (cilantro)
150 ml/¼ pint/⅔ cup single (light) cream

1 ▲ Peel the king prawns (jumbo shrimp) and cube the paneer.

2 Blend the tomato purée (paste), yogurt, garam masala, chilli powder, garlic, salt, mango powder and ground coriander in a mixing bowl and set to one side.

3 ▲ Melt the butter with the oil in a deep round-bottomed frying pan (skillet) or a medium karahi. Lower the heat slightly and quickly fry the paneer and prawns for about 2 minutes. Remove with a slotted spoon and drain on kitchen paper (paper towels).

4 ▲ Pour the spice mixture into the fat left in the pan and stir-fry for about 1 minute.

5 ▲ Add the paneer and prawns, and cook for 7–10 minutes, stirring occasionally, until the prawns are heated through.

6 ▲ Add the fresh chillies and most of the coriander (cilantro), and pour in the cream. Heat through for about 2 minutes, garnish with the remaining coriander and serve.

**HOME-MADE PANEER**

*To make paneer at home, bring 1 litre/1¾ pints/4 cups milk to the boil over a low heat. Add 2 tbsp lemon juice, stirring continuously and gently until the milk thickens and begins to curdle. Strain the curdled milk through a sieve (strainer) lined with muslin (cheesecloth). Set aside under a heavy weight for about 1½–2 hours to press to a flat shape about 1 cm/½ in thick.*

*Make the paneer a day before you plan to use it in a recipe; it will then be firmer and easier to handle. Cut and use as required; it will keep for about one week in the refrigerator.*

# Balti Prawns (Shrimp) in Hot Sauce

*This sizzling prawn (shrimp) dish is cooked in a fiery hot and spicy sauce. Not only does this sauce contain chilli powder, it is enhanced further by the addition of ground green chillies mixed with other spices. If the heat gets too much for anyone with a delicate palate, the addition of Raita will help to soften the piquant flavour.*

**SERVES 4**

**INGREDIENTS**

2 medium onions, roughly chopped
2 tbsp tomato purée (paste)
1 tsp ground coriander
¼ tsp turmeric
1 tsp chilli powder
2 medium fresh green chillies
3 tbsp chopped fresh coriander (cilantro)
2 tbsp lemon juice
1 tsp salt
3 tbsp corn oil
16 cooked king prawns (jumbo shrimp)
1 fresh green chilli, chopped (optional)

1 ▲ Put the onions, tomato purée (paste), ground coriander, turmeric, chilli powder, 2 whole green chillies, 2 tbsp of the fresh coriander (cilantro), the lemon juice and salt into the bowl of a food processor. Process for about 1 minute. If the mixture seems too thick, add a little water to loosen it.

2 ▲ Heat the oil in a deep round-bottomed frying pan (skillet) or a karahi. Lower the heat slightly and add the spice mixture. Fry the mixture for 3–5 minutes or until the sauce has thickened slightly.

3 ▲ Add the prawns (shrimp) and stir-fry quickly over a medium heat.

4 As soon as the prawns are heated through, transfer them to a serving dish and garnish with the rest of the fresh coriander and the chopped green chilli, if using. Serve immediately.

**COOK'S TIP**

*Cooked prawns (shrimp) have been used in all the seafood recipes. However, raw prawns – if you can find them – are especially delicious. Remove the black vein along the back of each prawn and extend the cooking time if necessary. The prawns will turn pink when they are cooked through.*

# Karahi Prawns (Shrimp) and Fenugreek

*The black-eyed peas, prawns (shrimp)
and paneer in this recipe mean that it is
rich in protein. The combination of both
ground and fresh fenugreek makes this a
very fragrant and delicious dish. When
preparing fresh fenugreek, use the leaves
whole, but discard the stalks which
would add a bitter flavour to the dish.*

**SERVES 4–6**

### INGREDIENTS
*4 tbsp corn oil*
*2 medium onions, sliced*
*2 medium tomatoes, sliced*
*1½ tsp garlic pulp*
*1 tsp chilli powder*
*1 tsp ginger pulp*
*1 tsp ground cumin*
*1 tsp ground coriander*
*1 tsp salt*
*150 g/5 oz paneer, cubed*
*1 tsp ground fenugreek*
*1 bunch fresh fenugreek leaves*
*115 g/4 oz cooked prawns (shrimp)*
*2 fresh red chillies, sliced*
*2 tbsp chopped fresh coriander (cilantro)*
*50 g/2 oz/⅓ cup canned black-eye peas,
    drained*
*1 tbsp lemon juice*

**2 ▲** Add the garlic, chilli powder,
ginger, ground cumin, ground
coriander, salt, paneer and the ground
and fresh fenugreek. Lower the heat
and stir-fry for about 2 minutes.

**3 ▲** Add the prawns (shrimp), red
chillies, fresh coriander (cilantro) and
the black-eyed peas and mix well. Cook
for a further 3–5 minutes, stirring
occasionally, or until the prawns are
heated through.

**4** Finally sprinkle on the lemon juice
and serve.

**1 ▲** Heat the oil in a deep round-
bottomed frying pan (skillet) or a
karahi. Lower the heat slightly and add
the onions and tomatoes. Fry for about
3 minutes.

# Seafood Balti with Vegetables

*In this dish, the spicy seafood is cooked separately and combined with the vegetables at the last minute to give a truly delicious combination of flavours.*

**SERVES 4**

**INGREDIENTS**
**Seafood**
*225 g/¹/₂ lb cod, or any other firm, white fish*
*225 g/¹/₂ lb cooked prawns (shrimp)*
*6 crab sticks, halved lengthways*
*1 tbsp lemon juice*
*1 tsp ground coriander*
*1 tsp chilli powder*
*1 tsp salt*
*1 tsp ground cumin*
*4 tbsp cornflour (cornstarch)*
*150 ml/¹/₄ pint/²/₃ cup corn oil*

**Vegetables**
*150 ml/¹/₄ pint/²/₃ cup corn oil*
*2 medium onions, chopped*
*1 tsp onion seeds*
*¹/₂ medium cauliflower, cut into florets (flowerets)*
*115 g/4 oz French (green) beans, cut into 2.5 cm/1 in lengths*
*175 g/6 oz/1 cup sweetcorn (corn kernels)*
*1 tsp shredded ginger*
*1 tsp chilli powder*
*1 tsp salt*
*4 fresh green chillies, sliced*
*2 tbsp chopped fresh coriander (cilantro)*
*lime slices*

1  Skin the fish and cut into small cubes. Put into a medium mixing bowl with the prawns (shrimps) and crab sticks, and put to one side.

2 ▲ In a separate bowl, mix together the lemon juice, ground coriander, chilli powder, salt and ground cumin. Pour this over the seafood and mix together thoroughly using your hands.

3  Sprinkle on the cornflour (cornstarch) and mix again until the seafood is well coated. Set to one side in the refrigerator for about 1 hour to allow the flavours to develop.

4 ▲ To make the vegetable mixture, heat the oil in a deep round-bottomed frying pan (skillet) or a karahi. Throw in the onions and the onion seeds, and stir-fry until lightly browned.

5  Add the cauliflower, French (green) beans, sweetcorn (corn kernels), ginger, chilli powder, salt, green chillies and fresh coriander (cilantro). Stir-fry for about 7–10 minutes over a medium heat, making sure that the cauliflower florets (flowerets) retain their shape.

6 ▲ Spoon the fried vegetables around the edge of a shallow dish, leaving a space in the middle for the seafood, and keep warm.

7 ▲ Wash and dry the pan, then heat the oil to fry the seafood pieces. Fry the seafood pieces in 2–3 batches, until they turn a golden brown. Remove with a slotted spoon and drain on kitchen paper (paper towels).

8  Arrange the seafood in the middle of the dish of vegetables and keep warm while you fry the remaining seafood. Garnish with lime slices and serve. Plain boiled rice and Raita make ideal accompaniments.

# Meat Dishes

*Both lamb and beef are eaten in Pakistan, although lamb is usually cooked for preference. In the Balti dishes described here, leg of lamb has usually been specified as it is less fatty and cooks more quickly, but equal portions of leg and shoulder can also be used if wished. Balti Lamb Tikka is one of the most popular Balti dishes, and there are two variations of this classic for you to try here, together with many other delicious choices.*

# Balti Lamb Tikka 1

*This is a traditional tikka recipe, in which the lamb is marinated in yogurt and spices. The lamb is usually cut into cubes, but the cooking time can be halved by cutting it into strips instead, as I have done in this recipe.*

**SERVES 4**

**INGREDIENTS**
450 g/1 lb lamb, cut into strips
175 ml/6 fl oz/³⁄₄ cup natural (plain)
    yogurt
1 tsp ground cumin
1 tsp ground coriander
1 tsp chilli powder
1 tsp garlic pulp
1 tsp salt
1 tsp garam masala
2 tbsp chopped fresh coriander (cilantro)
2 tbsp lemon juice
2 tbsp corn oil
1 tbsp tomato purée (tomato paste)
1 large green (bell) pepper, seeded and
    sliced
3 large fresh red chillies

1 ▲ Put the lamb strips, yogurt, ground cumin, ground coriander, chilli powder, garlic, salt, garam masala, fresh coriander (cilantro) and lemon juice into a large mixing bowl and stir thoroughly. Set to one side for at least 1 hour to marinate.

2 ▲ Heat the oil in a deep round-bottomed frying pan (skillet) or a medium karahi. Lower the heat slightly and add the tomato purée (paste).

3 ▲ Add the lamb strips to the pan, a few at a time, leaving any excess marinade behind in the bowl.

4 Cook the lamb, stirring frequently, for 7–10 minutes or until it is well browned.

5 ▲ Finally, add the green (bell) pepper slices and the whole red chillies. Heat through, checking that the lamb is cooked through, and serve.

# Balti Minced (Ground) Lamb with Potatoes and Fenugreek

*The combination of lamb with fresh fenugreek works very well in this dish, which is delicious accompanied by plain boiled rice and mango pickle. Only use the fenugreek leaves, as the stalks can be rather bitter. This dish is traditionally served with rice.*

**SERVES 4**

**INGREDIENTS**

450 g/1 lb lean minced (ground) lamb
1 tsp ginger pulp
1 tsp garlic pulp
1¹/₂ tsp chilli powder
1 tsp salt
¹/₄ tsp turmeric
3 tbsp corn oil
2 medium onions, sliced
2 medium potatoes, peeled, par-boiled and
    roughly diced
1 bunch fresh fenugreek, chopped
2 tomatoes, chopped
50 g/2 oz/¹/₂ cup frozen peas
2 tbsp chopped fresh coriander (cilantro)
3 fresh red chillies, seeded and sliced

1 ▲ Put the minced (ground) lamb, ginger, garlic, chilli powder, salt and turmeric into a large bowl, and mix together thoroughly. Set to one side.

2 Heat the oil in a deep round-bottomed frying pan (skillet) or a medium karahi. Throw in the onion and fry for about 5 minutes until golden brown.

3 ▲ Add the minced lamb and stir-fry over a medium heat for 5–7 minutes.

4 ▲ Stir in the potatoes, chopped fenugreek, tomatoes and peas and cook for a further 5–7 minutes, stirring continuously.

5 Just before serving, stir in the fresh coriander (cilantro) and garnish with fresh red chillies.

# Balti Lamb Tikka 2

*One of the best ways of tenderizing meat is to marinate it in papaya, which must be unripe or it will lend its sweetness to what should be a savory dish. Papaya, or paw-paw, is readily available from most large supermarkets.*

**SERVES 4**

❖❖❖❖❖❖❖❖❖❖❖❖❖❖❖❖❖❖❖❖❖

INGREDIENTS
675 g/1½ lb lean lamb, cubed
1 unripe papaya
3 tbsp natural (plain) yogurt
1 tsp ginger pulp
1 tsp chilli powder
1 tsp garlic pulp
¼ tsp turmeric
2 tsp ground coriander
1 tsp ground cumin
1 tsp salt
2 tbsp lemon juice
1 tbsp chopped fresh coriander (cilantro),
    plus extra to garnish
¼ tsp red food colouring
300 ml/½ pint/1¼ cups corn oil
lemon wedges
onion rings

❖❖❖❖❖❖❖❖❖❖❖❖❖❖❖❖❖❖❖❖❖

I ▲ Place the lamb in a large mixing bowl. Peel the papaya, cut in half and scoop out the seeds. Cut the flesh into cubes and blend in a food processor or blender until it is pulped, adding about 1 tbsp water if necessary.

2 ▲ Pour 2 tbsp of the papaya pulp over the lamb cubes and rub it in well with your fingers. Set to one side for at least 3 hours.

3 ▲ Meanwhile, mix together the yogurt, ginger, chilli powder, garlic, turmeric, ground coriander, ground cumin, salt, lemon juice, fresh coriander (cilantro), red food colouring and 2 tbsp of the oil, and set to one side.

4 ▲ Pour the spicy yogurt mixture over the lamb and mix together well.

5 ▲ Heat the remaining oil in a deep round-bottomed frying pan (skillet) or a karahi. Lower the heat slightly and add the lamb cubes, a few at a time.

6   Deep-fry each batch for 5–7 minutes or until the lamb is thoroughly cooked and tender. Keep the cooked pieces warm while the remainder is fried.

7   Transfer to a serving dish and garnish with lemon wedges, onion rings and fresh coriander. Serve with Raita and freshly baked Naan.

**COOK'S TIP**

❖❖❖❖❖❖❖❖❖❖❖❖❖❖❖❖❖❖❖❖❖

*A good-quality meat tenderizer, available from supermarkets, can be used in place of the papaya. However, the meat will need a longer marinating time and should ideally be left to tenderize overnight.*

# Balti Minced (Ground) Lamb Koftas with Vegetables

*These koftas look most attractive served on their bed of vegetables, especially if you make them quite small.*

**SERVES 4**

**INGREDIENTS**

**Koftas**
*450 g/1 lb lean minced (ground) lamb*
*1 tsp garam masala*
*1 tsp ground cumin*
*1 tsp ground coriander*
*1 tsp garlic pulp*
*1 tsp chilli powder*
*1 tsp salt*
*1 tbsp chopped fresh coriander (cilantro)*
*1 small onion, finely diced*
*150 ml/¼ pint/⅔ cup corn oil*

**Vegetables**
*3 tbsp corn oil*
*1 bunch spring onions (scallions), roughly*
  *chopped*
*½ large red (bell) pepper, seeded and*
  *chopped*
*½ large green (bell) pepper, seeded and*
  *chopped*
*175 g/6 oz/1 cup sweetcorn (corn kernels)*
*225 g/8 oz/1½ cups canned butter beans,*
  *drained*
*½ small cauliflower, cut into florets*
  *(flowerets)*
*4 fresh green chillies, chopped*

*1 tsp chopped fresh mint*
*1 tbsp chopped fresh coriander (cilantro)*
*1 tbsp shredded ginger*
*lime slices*
*1 tbsp lemon juice*

1 Put the minced (ground) lamb into a food processor or blender and process for about 1 minute.

2 ▲ Transfer the lamb into a medium bowl. Add the garam masala, ground cumin, ground coriander, garlic, chilli powder, salt, fresh coriander (cilantro) and onion, and use your fingers to blend everything thoroughly.

3 Cover the bowl and set aside in the refrigerator.

4 ▲ Heat the oil for the vegetables in a deep round-bottomed frying pan (skillet) or a medium karahi. Add the spring onions (scallions) and stir-fry for about 2 minutes.

5 ▲ Add the (bell) peppers, sweetcorn (corn kernels), butter beans, cauliflower and green chillies, and stir-fry over a high heat for about 2 minutes. Set to one side.

6 ▲ Using your hands, roll small pieces of the kofta mixture into golf-ball sized portions. It should make between 12 and 16 koftas.

7 ▲ Heat the oil for the koftas in a frying pan. Lower the heat slightly and add the koftas, a few at a time. Shallow-fry each batch, turning the koftas, until they are evenly browned.

8 Remove from the oil with a slotted spoon, and drain on kitchen paper (paper towels).

9 ▲ Put the vegetable mixture back over a medium heat, and add the cooked koftas. Stir the mixture gently for about 5 minutes, or until everything is heated through.

10 Garnish with the mint, coriander, shredded ginger and lime slices. Just before serving, sprinkle over the lemon juice.

# Lamb with Spinach

*Lamb with Spinach, or Saag Goshth, is a well-known recipe from the Punjab, and a great favourite of mine. It is important to use red (bell) peppers as they add such a distinctive flavour to the dish. Serve with plain boiled rice, Naan or Paratha.*

**SERVES 4–6**

INGREDIENTS
*1 tsp ginger pulp*
*1 tsp garlic pulp*
*1½ tsp chilli powder*
*1 tsp salt*
*1 tsp garam masala*
*6 tbsp corn oil*
*2 medium onions, sliced*
*675 g/1½ lb lean lamb, cut into 5 cm/2 in cubes*
*600–900 ml/1–1½ pints/2½–3¾ cups water*
*400 g/14 oz fresh spinach*
*1 large red (bell) pepper, seeded and chopped*
*3 fresh green chillies, chopped*
*3 tbsp chopped fresh coriander (cilantro)*
*1 tbsp lemon juice (optional)*

1 Mix together the ginger, garlic, chilli powder, salt and garam masala in a bowl. Set to one side.

2 Heat the oil in a medium saucepan. Add the onions and fry for 10–12 minutes or until well browned.

3 Add the cubed lamb to the sizzling onions and stir-fry for about 2 minutes.

4 ▲ Tip in the spice mixture and stir thoroughly until the meat pieces are well coated.

5 Pour in the water and bring to the boil. As soon as it is boiling, cover the pan and lower the heat. Cook gently for 25–35 minutes without letting the contents of the pan burn.

6 ▲ If there is still a lot of water in the pan when the meat has become tender, remove the lid and boil briskly to evaporate any excess.

7 ▲ Meanwhile, wash and chop the spinach roughly before blanching it for about 1 minute in a pan of boiling water. Drain well.

8 ▲ Add the spinach to the lamb as soon as the water has evaporated. Fry over a medium heat for 7–10 minutes, using a wooden spoon in a semi-circular motion, scraping the bottom of the pan as you stir.

9 ▲ Add the red (bell) pepper, green chillies and fresh coriander (cilantro) to the pan and stir over a medium heat for 2 minutes. Sprinkle on the lemon juice (if using) and serve immediately.

**COOK'S TIP**

*Frozen spinach can also be used for the dish, but try to find whole leaf spinach rather than the chopped kind. Allow the frozen spinach to thaw, then drain well; there is no need to blanch it.*

# Khara Masala Lamb

*Whole spices (khara) are used in this curry so you should warn the diners of their presence! Delicious served with freshly baked Naan or a rice accompaniment, this dish is best made with good-quality spring lamb.*

**SERVES 4**

INGREDIENTS
5 tbsp corn oil
2 medium onions, chopped
1 tsp shredded ginger
1 tsp sliced garlic
6 whole dried red chillies
3 cardamom pods
2 cinnamon sticks
6 black peppercorns
3 cloves
1/2 tsp salt
450 g/1 lb boned leg of lamb, cubed
600 ml/1 pint/2 1/2 cups water
2 fresh green chillies, sliced
2 tbsp chopped fresh coriander (cilantro)

1   Heat the oil in a large saucepan. Lower the heat slightly and fry the onions until they are lightly browned.

2 ▲ Add half the ginger and half the garlic and stir well.

3 ▲ Throw in half the red chillies, the cardamoms, cinnamon, peppercorns, cloves and salt.

4 ▲ Add the lamb and fry over a medium heat. Stir continuously with a semi-circular movement, using a wooden spoon to scrape the bottom of the pan. Continue in this way for about 5 minutes.

5   Pour in the water, cover with a lid and cook over a medium-low heat for 35–40 minutes, or until the water has evaporated and the meat is tender.

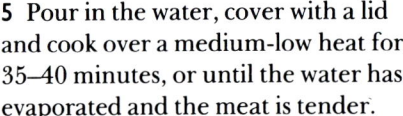

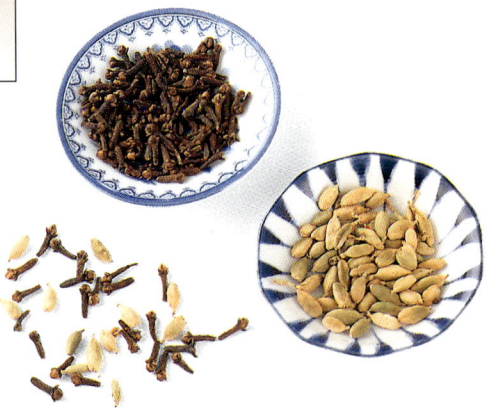

6 ▲ Add the rest of the ginger, garlic and dried red chillies, along with the fresh green chillies and fresh coriander (cilantro).

7 ▲ Continue to stir over the heat until you see some free oil on the sides of the pan. Transfer to a serving dish and serve immediately.

**COOK'S TIP**

*The action of stirring the meat and spices together using a semi-circular motion, as described in step 4, is called bhoono-ing. It ensures that the meat becomes well-coated and combined with the spice mixture before the cooking liquid is added.*

# Balti Mini Lamb Kebabs (Kabobs) with Baby Onions

*This is rather an unusual Balti dish as the kebabs (kabobs) are first grilled (broiled) before being added to the karahi for the final stage of cooking.*

**SERVES 6**

INGREDIENTS
*450 g/1 lb lean minced (ground) lamb*
*1 medium onion, finely chopped*
*1 tsp garam masala*
*1 tsp garlic pulp*
*2 medium fresh green chillies, finely*
  *chopped*
*2 tbsp chopped fresh coriander (cilantro)*
*1 tsp salt*
*1 tbsp plain (all-purpose) flour*
*4 tbsp corn oil*
*12 baby onions*
*4 fresh green chillies, sliced*
*12 cherry tomatoes*
*2 tbsp chopped fresh coriander*

I ▲ Blend together the minced (ground) lamb, onion, garam masala, garlic, green chillies, fresh coriander (cilantro), salt and flour in a medium bowl. Use your hands to make sure that all the ingredients are thoroughly mixed together.

2  Transfer the mixture to a food processor and process for about 1 minute, to make the mixture even finer in texture.

3 ▲ Put the mixture back into the bowl. Break off small pieces, about the size of a lime, and wrap them around skewers to form small sausage shapes. Put about 2 kebabs (kabobs) on each skewer.

4 ▲ Once you have used up all the mixture, baste the kebabs with 1 tbsp of the oil and place under a preheated hot grill (broiler) for 12–15 minutes, turning and basting occasionally, until they are evenly browned.

5 ▲ Heat the remaining 3 tbsp of the oil in a deep round-bottomed frying pan (skillet) or a medium karahi. Lower the heat slightly and add the whole baby onions. As soon as they start to darken, add the fresh chillies and tomatoes.

6 ▲ Remove the mini kebabs from their skewers and add them to the onion and tomato mixture. Stir gently for about 3 minutes to heat them through.

7  Transfer to a serving dish and garnish with fresh coriander. Serve with Spicy Balti Potatoes and Paratha.

# Lamb Chops Kashmiri-Style

*These chops are cooked in a unique way, being first boiled in milk, and then fried. Despite the large number of spices used in this recipe, the actual dish has a mild flavour, and is delicious served with fried rice and a lentil dish.*

**SERVES 4**

**INGREDIENTS**

*8–12 lamb chops, about 50–75 g/2–3 oz each*
*1 piece cinnamon bark*
*1 bay leaf*
*½ tsp fennel seeds*
*½ tsp black peppercorns*
*3 green cardamom pods*
*1 tsp salt*
*600 ml/1 pint/2½ cups milk*
*150 ml/¼ pint/⅔ cup evaporated milk*
*150 ml/¼ pint/⅔ cup natural (plain) yogurt*
*2 tbsp plain (all-purpose) flour*
*1 tsp chilli powder*
*1 tsp ginger pulp*
*½ tsp garam masala*
*½ tsp garlic pulp*
*pinch of salt*
*300 ml/½ pint/1¼ cups corn oil*
*mint sprigs*
*lime quarters*

1 ▲ Trim the lamb chops and place them in a large saucepan with the cinnamon bark, bay leaf, fennel seeds, peppercorns, cardamoms, salt and milk. Bring to the boil over a high heat.

2 ▲ Lower the heat and cook for 12–15 minutes, or until the milk has reduced to about half its original volume. At this stage, add the evaporated milk and lower the heat further. Simmer until the chops are cooked through and the milk has evaporated.

3 ▲ While the chops are cooking, blend together the yogurt, flour, chilli powder, ginger, garam masala, garlic and a pinch of salt in a mixing bowl.

4 ▲ Remove the chops from the saucepan and discard the whole spices. Add the chops to the spicy yogurt mixture.

5 ▲ Heat the oil in a deep round-bottomed frying pan (skillet) or medium karahi. Lower the heat slightly and add the chops. Fry until they are golden brown, turning them once or twice as they cook.

6 Transfer to a serving dish, and garnish with mint sprigs and lime quarters.

**COOK'S TIP**

*These delicious lamb chops, with their crunchy yogurt coating, make ideal finger food to serve at a buffet or drinks party.*

# Lentils with Lamb and Tomatoes

*This dish is full of protein and has a deliciously light texture. Serve with Colourful Pullao Rice.*

## SERVES 4

### INGREDIENTS

*4 tbsp corn oil*
*1 bay leaf*
*2 cloves*
*4 black peppercorns*
*1 medium onion, sliced*
*450 g/1 lb lean lamb, boned and cubed*
*1/4 tsp turmeric*
*1 1/2 tsp chilli powder*
*1 tsp crushed coriander seeds*
*2.5 cm/1 in cinnamon stick*
*1 tsp garlic pulp*
*1 1/2 tsp salt*
*1.5 litres/2 1/2 pints/6 1/4 cups water*
*50 g/2 oz/1/3 cup round yellow lentils
    (chana dhal), or yellow split peas*
*2 medium tomatoes, quartered*
*2 fresh green chillies, chopped*
*1 tbsp chopped fresh coriander (cilantro)*

1 ▲ Heat the oil in a deep round-bottomed frying pan (skillet) or a karahi. Lower the heat slightly and add the bay leaf, cloves, peppercorns and onion. Fry for about 5 minutes, or until the onions are golden brown.

2 ▲ Add the cubed lamb, turmeric, chilli powder, coriander seeds, cinnamon stick, garlic and most of the salt, and stir-fry for about 5 minutes over a medium heat.

3  Pour in 900 ml/1 1/2 pints/3 3/4 cups of the water and cover the pan with a lid or foil, making sure the foil does not come into contact with the food. Simmer over a low heat for about 35–40 minutes, or until the water has evaporated and the lamb is tender.

4  Put the lentils into a saucepan with 600 ml/1 pint/2 1/2 cups water and boil for about 12–15 minutes, or until the water has almost evaporated and the lentils are soft enough to be easily mashed. If the lentils are too thick, add up to 150 ml/1/4 pint/2/3 cup water to loosen them.

5 ▲ When the lamb is tender, stir-fry the mixture using a wooden spoon, until some free oil begins to appear on the sides of the pan.

6 ▲ Add the cooked lentils to the lamb and mix together well.

7 ▲ Add the tomatoes, chillies and fresh coriander (cilantro) and serve.

## COOK'S TIP

*Boned and cubed chicken can be used in place of the lamb. At step 3, reduce the amount of water to 300 ml/1/2 pint/1 1/4 cups and cook uncovered, stirring occasionally, for 10–15 minutes or until the water has evaporated and the chicken is cooked through.*

# Lamb Pullao

*A pullao is a rice dish containing whole spices, which can either be plain or combined with meat, chicken or vegetables. Here it is made with minced (ground) lamb cooked in yogurt with a variety of spices. It makes a complete meal served on its own or served with Raita.*

**SERVES 4–6**

INGREDIENTS

*2 tbsp corn oil*
*1 tbsp unsalted butter or ghee*
*2 medium onions, sliced*
*1 tsp garlic pulp*
*1 tsp chilli powder*
*¼ tsp ginger pulp*
*¼ tsp turmeric*
*1 tsp garam masala*
*1 tsp salt*
*2 tbsp natural (plain) yogurt*
*2 medium tomatoes, sliced*
*450 g/1 lb lean minced (ground) lamb*
*2 tbsp chopped fresh coriander (cilantro)*
*2 medium fresh chillies, chopped*
*tomato slices (optional)*

## Rice

*450 g/1 lb/2¼ cups basmati rice*
*1.2 litres/2 pints/5 cups water*
*4 cloves*
*4 green cardamom pods*
*½ tsp black cumin seeds*
*6 black peppercorns*
*1½ tsp salt*
*1 tbsp chopped fresh coriander*
*2 fresh green chillies, chopped*
*1 tbsp lime juice*
*½ tsp saffron strands soaked in 2 tbsp milk (optional)*

1  Wash the rice twice, drain and set aside in a sieve (strainer).

2  Heat the oil and ghee in a deep round-bottomed frying pan (skillet) or a large karahi. Add the onions and fry until golden brown.

3 ▲ Lower the heat to medium and add the garlic, chilli powder, ginger, turmeric, garam masala, salt, yogurt and tomatoes and stir-fry gently for about 1 minute.

4 ▲ Add the minced (ground) lamb and turn up the heat to high. Use a slotted spoon to fry the lamb, scraping the bottom of the pan to prevent it from burning.

5 ▲ Add the fresh coriander (cilantro) and chillies, and continue to stir, breaking up any lumps in the meat as you work. Once the lamb is throughly cooked, set it to one side.

6  Put the rice into a large saucepan with the water, cloves, cardamoms, cumin seeds, peppercorns and salt, and bring to boil. When the rice has boiled for 2 minutes, drain off the water along with half the rice, leaving the rest in the saucepan.

7 ▲ Spread the cooked lamb over the rice in the saucepan and cover with the rice left in the strainer.

8 ▲ Add the fresh coriander, green chillies, lime juice and saffron in milk if using.

9  Cover the saucepan with a tight-fitting lid and cook over a very low heat for 15–20 minutes.

10 ▲ Check that the rice is cooked through and mix gently with a slotted spoon before serving. Garnish with slices of tomato if wished.

# Vegetable Dishes

*Pakistan is a meat-eating nation, so vegetables are usually cooked as side dishes rather than as a main dish. The vegetables are bought fresh from local markets and stalls on a daily basis, so only seasonal varieties are available. In the West, we have a wide choice of vegetables, including exotica, all year round. The Balti dishes chosen for this chapter make extensive use of baby vegetables, which taste delicious and look especially attractive.*

# Balti Baby Vegetables

*There is a wide and wonderful selection of baby vegetables available in supermarkets these days, and this simple recipe does full justice to their delicate flavour and attractive appearance. Serve as part of a main meal or even as a light appetizer.*

**SERVES 4–6**

INGREDIENTS
*10 new potatoes, halved*
*12–14 baby carrots*
*12–14 baby courgettes (zucchini)*
*2 tbsp corn oil*
*15 baby onions*
*2 tbsp chilli sauce*
*1 tsp garlic pulp*
*1 tsp ginger pulp*
*1 tsp salt*
*400 g/14 oz/2 cups canned chick-peas (garbanzos), drained*
*10 cherry tomatoes*
*1 tsp crushed dried red chillies*
*2 tbsp sesame seeds*

1 ▲ Bring a medium pan of salted water to the boil and add the potatoes and carrots. After about 12–15 minutes, add the courgettes (zucchini) and boil for a further 5 minutes or until all the vegetables are just tender.

2 ▲ Drain the vegetables well and set to one side.

3 ▲ Heat the oil in a deep round-bottomed frying pan (skillet) or a karahi and add the baby onions. Fry until the onions turn golden brown. Lower the heat and add the chilli sauce, garlic, ginger and salt, taking care not to burn the mixture.

4 ▲ Add the chick-peas (garbanzos) and stir-fry over a medium heat until the moisture has been absorbed.

5 ▲ Add the cooked vegetables and cherry tomatoes and stir over the heat with a slotted spoon for about 2 minutes.

6 Add the crushed red chillies and sesame seeds as a garnish and serve.

**VARIATION**

*By varying the vegetables chosen and experimenting with different combinations, this recipe can form the basis for a wide variety of vegetable accompaniments. Try baby corn cobs, French (green) beans, mange-tout (snow peas), okra and cauliflower florets (flowerets), too.*

# Balti Stuffed Vegetables

*Aubergines (eggplants) and (bell) peppers make an excellent combination. Here they are stuffed with an aromatic lamb filling and served on a bed of sautéed onions.*

**SERVES 6**

INGREDIENTS
*3 small aubergines (eggplants)*
*1 each red, green and yellow (bell) peppers*

**Stuffing**
*3 tbsp corn oil*
*3 medium onions, sliced*
*1 tsp chilli powder*
*¼ tsp turmeric*
*1 tsp ground coriander*
*1 tsp ground cumin*
*1 tsp ginger pulp*
*1 tsp garlic pulp*
*1 tsp salt*
*450 g/1 lb lean minced (ground) lamb*
*3 fresh green chillies, chopped*
*2 tbsp chopped fresh coriander (cilantro)*

**Sautéed onions**
*3 tbsp corn oil*
*1 tsp mixed onion, mustard, fenugreek and white cumin seeds*
*4 dried red chillies*
*3 medium onions, roughly chopped*
*1 tsp salt*
*1 tsp chilli powder*
*2 medium tomatoes, sliced*
*2 fresh green chillies, chopped*
*2 tbsp chopped fresh coriander*

I Prepare the vegetables. Slit the aubergines (eggplants) lengthways up to the stalks; keep the stalks intact. Cut the tops off the (bell) peppers and remove the seeds. You can retain the pepper tops and use them as 'lids' once the vegetables have been stuffed, if wished.

2 Make the stuffing. Heat the oil in a medium saucepan. Add the onions and fry for about 3 minutes. Lower the heat and add the chilli powder, turmeric, ground coriander, ground cumin, ginger, garlic and salt, and stir-fry for about 1 minute. Add the minced (ground) lamb to the pan and turn up the heat.

3 ▲ Stir-fry for 7–10 minutes or until the mince is cooked, using a wooden spoon to scrape the bottom of the pan. Throw in the green chillies and fresh coriander (cilantro) towards the end. Remove from the heat, cover and set to one side.

4 Make the sautéed onions. Heat the oil in a deep round-bottomed frying pan (skillet) or a karahi and throw in the mixed onion, mustard, fenugreek and white cumin seeds together with the dried red chillies, and fry for about 1 minute. Add the onions and fry for about 2 minutes or until soft.

5 Add the salt, chilli powder, tomatoes, green chillies and fresh coriander. Cook for a further minute. Remove from the heat and set to one side.

6 ▲ The minced lamb should by now be cool enough to stuff the prepared aubergines and peppers. Fill the vegetables quite loosely with the meat mixture.

7 ▲ As you stuff the vegetables, place them on top of the sautéed onions in the karahi. Cover with foil, making sure the foil doesn't touch the food, and cook over a low heat for about 15 minutes.

8 The dish is ready as soon as the aubergines and peppers are tender. Serve with a dish of plain boiled rice or Colourful Pullao Rice.

**VARIATION**

*Large beef tomatoes are also delicious stuffed with the lightly spiced lamb mixture. Simply cut off the tops and scoop out the cores, seeds and some of the pulp and cook as described above.*

# Spiced Potatoes and Carrots Parisienne

*Ready prepared "parisienne" vegetables have recently become available in many supermarkets. These are simply root vegetables that have been peeled and cut into perfectly spherical shapes. This dish looks extremely fresh and appetizing and is equally delicious.*

**SERVES 4**

INGREDIENTS
*175 g/6 oz carrots parisienne*
*175 g/6 oz potatoes parisienne*
*115 g/4 oz runner beans, sliced*
*75 g/3 oz/6 tbsp butter*
*1 tbsp corn oil*
*¼ tsp onion seeds*
*¼ tsp fenugreek seeds*
*4 dried red chillies*
*½ tsp mustard seeds*
*6 curry leaves*
*1 medium onion, sliced*
*1 tsp salt*

*4 garlic cloves, sliced*
*4 fresh red chillies*
*1 tbsp chopped fresh coriander (cilantro)*
*1 tbsp chopped fresh mint*
*mint sprig*

I ▲ Drop the carrots, potatoes and runner beans into a pan of boiling water, and cook for about 7 minutes, or until they are just tender but not overcooked. Drain and set to one side.

2 ▲ Heat the butter and oil in a deep round-bottomed frying pan (skillet) or a large karahi and add the onion seeds, fenugreek seeds, dried red chillies, mustard seeds and curry leaves. When these have sizzled for a few seconds, add the onion and fry for 3–5 minutes.

3 ▲ Add the salt, garlic and fresh chillies, followed by the cooked vegetables, and stir gently for about 5 minutes, over a medium heat.

4  Add the fresh coriander (cilantro) and mint and serve hot garnished with a sprig of mint.

# Karahi Shredded Cabbage with Cumin

*This cabbage dish is only lightly spiced and makes a good accompaniment to most other dishes.*

**SERVES 4**

INGREDIENTS
*1 tbsp corn oil*
*50 g/2 oz/4 tbsp butter*
*½ tsp crushed coriander seeds*
*½ tsp white cumin seeds*
*6 dried red chillies*
*1 small savoy cabbage, shredded*
*12 mange-tout (snow peas)*
*3 fresh red chillies, seeded and sliced*
*12 baby corn cobs*
*salt, to taste*
*25 g/1 oz/¼ cup flaked (slivered)*
  *almonds, toasted*
*1 tbsp chopped fresh coriander (cilantro)*

1  Heat the oil and butter in a deep round-bottomed frying pan (skillet) or a karahi and add the crushed coriander seeds, white cumin seeds and dried red chillies.

2 ▲ Add the shredded cabbage and mange-tout (snow peas) and stir-fry for about 5 minutes.

3 ▲ Finally add the fresh red chillies, baby corn cobs and salt, and fry for a further 3 minutes.

4  Garnish with the toasted almonds and fresh coriander (cilantro), and serve hot.

# Spicy Balti Potatoes

**SERVES 4**

### INGREDIENTS
3 tbsp corn oil
1/2 tsp white cumin seeds
3 curry leaves
1 tsp crushed dried red chillies
1/2 tsp mixed onion, mustard and
   fenugreek seeds
1/2 tsp fennel seeds
3 garlic cloves
1/2 tsp shredded ginger
2 medium onions, sliced
6 new potatoes, cut into 5 mm/1/4 in slices
1 tbsp chopped fresh coriander (cilantro)
1 fresh red chilli, seeded and sliced
1 fresh green chilli, seeded and sliced

1 ▲ Heat the oil in a deep round-bottomed frying pan (skillet) or a karahi. Lower the heat slightly and add the cumin seeds, curry leaves, dried red chillies, mixed onion, mustard and fenugreek seeds, fennel seeds, garlic cloves and ginger. Fry for about 1 minute, then add the onions and fry for 5 minutes or until the onions are golden brown.

2 ▲ Add the potatoes, fresh coriander (cilantro) and fresh red and green chillies and mix well. Cover the pan tightly with a lid or foil, making sure the foil does not touch the food. Cook over a very low heat for about 7 minutes or until the potatoes are tender.

3 Remove the foil and serve hot.

# Okra with Green Mango and Lentils

*If you like okra, you'll love this spicy and tangy dish.*

**SERVES 4**

### INGREDIENTS
115 g/4 oz/2/3 cup yellow lentils (toor
   dhal)
3 tbsp corn oil
1/2 tsp onion seeds
2 medium onions, sliced
1/2 tsp ground fenugreek
1 tsp ginger pulp
1 tsp garlic pulp
1 1/2 tsp chilli powder
1/4 tsp turmeric
1 tsp ground coriander
1 green (unripe) mango, peeled and sliced
450 g/1 lb okra, cut into 1 cm/1/2 in pieces
1 1/2 tsp salt
2 fresh red chillies, seeded and sliced
2 tbsp chopped fresh coriander (cilantro)
1 tomato, sliced

1 ▲ Wash the lentils thoroughly and put in a saucepan with enough water to cover. Bring to the boil and cook until soft but not mushy. Drain and set to one side.

2 Heat the oil in a deep round-bottomed frying pan (skillet) or a karahi and fry the onion seeds until they begin to pop. Add the onions and fry until golden brown. Lower the heat and add the ground fenugreek, ginger, garlic, chilli powder, turmeric and ground coriander.

3 ▲ Throw in the mango slices and the okra. Stir well and add the salt, red chillies and fresh coriander (cilantro). Stir-fry for about 3 minutes or until the okra is well cooked.

4 Finally, add the cooked lentils and sliced tomato and cook for a further 3 minutes. Serve hot.

*Spicy Balti Potatoes (top) and Okra with Green Mango and Lentils*

# Breads, Rice & Side Dishes

*Some form of bread or rice is served with almost every meal on the Indian sub-continent — the meal would not be considered complete without one or other. Rice is cooked in a variety of ways: plain boiled rice is probably the most common, although pullao rice — cooked with spices, herbs, food colours or any of the proteins — is also very popular. Naan and paratha breads are often used to scoop up the contents of the Balti pan, or karahi, and to mop up the delicious sauces.*

# Paratha

*Paratha is an unleavened bread with rich, flaky layers. The preparation time is quite lengthy and, as parathas are best served fresh from the pan, you will need to plan your menu well ahead. They are fried rather than grilled (broiled) or baked and can be served as an accompaniment to almost any Balti dish.*

**MAKES ABOUT 8**

INGREDIENTS

*225 g/8 oz/1½ cups chapati (ata) flour
   (or use wholemeal/whole-wheat flour),
   plus extra for dusting*
*½ tsp salt*
*200 ml/7 fl oz/scant 1 cup water*
*115 g/4 oz/4 tbsp vegetable ghee, melted*

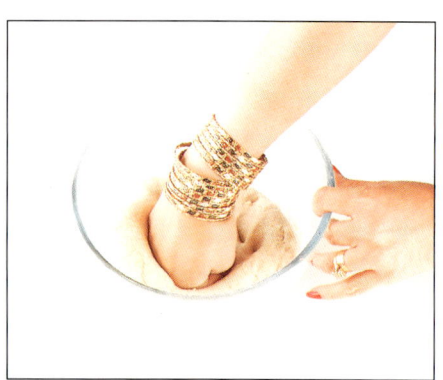

1 ▲ Put the flour and salt into a large mixing bowl. Make a well in the middle and add the water a little at a time, to make a soft but pliable dough. Knead well for a few minutes, then cover and leave to rest for about 1 hour.

2 ▲ Divide the dough into 8 even portions. Roll each one out on a lightly-floured surface into a round about 10 cm/4 in in diameter. Brush the middle with about ½ tsp ghee.

3 ▲ Fold in half and roll up into a tube.

4 ▲ Flatten slightly between your palms, then roll around your finger to form a coil. Roll out once again into a round about 18 cm/7 in in diameter, dusting with extra flour as necessary.

5 ▲ Heat a heavy-bottomed frying pan (skillet) and slap a paratha on to it. Move it gently around the pan to ensure that it is evenly exposed to the heat. Turn it over and brush with about 1 tsp of the ghee.

6 ▲ Cook for about 1 minute, then turn it over once again and cook for about 30 seconds, moving it around constantly.

7 Remove from the pan and keep warm, wrapped in foil. Fry the remaining parathas in the same way. Serve warm.

# Naan

*There are many ways of making naan bread, but this method is particularly easy to follow. Naans should be served warm, preferably straight from the grill (broiler).*

**MAKES ABOUT 6**

**INGREDIENTS**

*1 tsp caster (superfine) sugar*
*1 tsp dried (active dry) yeast*
*150 ml/¼ pint/⅔ cup warm water*
*225 g/8 oz/2 cups plain (all-purpose)*
  *flour, plus extra for dusting*
*1 tsp ghee, melted*
*1 tsp salt*
*50 g/2 oz/4 tbsp unsalted butter, melted*
*1 tsp poppy seeds*

**1** ▲ Put the sugar and yeast into a small bowl and add the warm water. Mix well until the yeast has dissolved, and leave on one side for about 10 minutes, or until the mixture has frothed up.

**2** ▲ Place the flour in a large mixing bowl, make a well in the middle and add the melted ghee, salt and the yeast mixture.

**3** ▲ Mix well, using your hands, and adding a little more water if the dough is too dry.

**4** ▲ Turn the dough out onto a lightly-floured surface and knead for about 5 minutes, or until smooth.

**5** ▲ Put the dough back into the bowl, cover and leave in a warm place for about 1½ hours, or until it has doubled in size.

**6** ▲ Turn out the dough back onto a floured surface and knead for a further 2 minutes.

**7** ▲ Break off small pieces of the dough with your hand, and roll into rounds about 13 cm/5 in in diameter and 1 cm/½ in thick.

**8** Place the naans on a sheet of greased foil under a very hot, preheated grill (broiler) for about 7–10 minutes, turning twice to brush with butter and sprinkle with poppy seeds.

**9** Serve immediately if possible, or keep wrapped in foil until required.

**COOK'S TIP**

*Onions seeds or fresh chopped coriander (cilantro) make an equally delicious topping in place of poppy seeds.*

# Colourful Pullao Rice

*This lightly spiced rice makes an extremely attractive accompaniment to many Balti dishes, and is easily made.*

**SERVES 4–6**

INGREDIENTS
*450 g/1 lb/2⅓ cups basmati rice*
*75 g/3 oz/6 tbsp unsalted butter*
*4 cloves*
*4 green cardamom pods*
*1 bay leaf*
*1 tsp salt*
*1 litre/1¾ pints/4 cups water*
*a few drops each of yellow, green and red food colouring*

1 Wash the rice twice, drain and set aside in a sieve (strainer).

2 ▲ Melt the butter in a medium saucepan, and throw in the cloves, cardamoms, bay leaf and salt. Lower the heat and add the rice. Fry for about 1 minute, stirring constantly.

3 Add the water and bring to the boil. As soon as it has boiled, cover the pan and reduce the heat. Cook for 15–20 minutes.

4 ▲ Just before you are ready to serve the rice, pour a few drops of each colouring at different sides of the pan. Leave to stand for 5 minutes, mix gently and serve.

# Fruity Pullao

**SERVES 4–6**

INGREDIENTS
*450 g/1 lb/2⅓ cups basmati rice*
*75 g/3 oz/6 tbsp unsalted butter*
*1 tbsp corn oil*
*1 bay leaf*
*6 black peppercorns*
*4 green cardamom pods*
*1 tsp salt*
*75 g/3 oz/½ cup sultanas (golden raisins)*
*50 g/2 oz/½ cup flaked (slivered) almonds*
*1 litre/1¾ pints/4 cups water*

1 Wash the rice twice, drain and set aside in a sieve (strainer).

2 ▲ Heat the butter and oil in a medium saucepan. Lower the heat and throw in the bay leaf, peppercorns and cardamoms, and fry for about 30 seconds.

3 ▲ Add the rice, salt, sultanas (golden raisins) and flaked (slivered) almonds. Stir-fry for about 1 minute, then pour in the water. Bring to the boil, then cover with a tightly-fitting lid and lower the heat. Cook for 15–20 minutes.

4 Turn off the heat and leave the rice to stand, still covered, for about 5 minutes before serving.

*Colourful Pullao Rice (top) and Fruity Pullao*

# Raita

*Raita is very versatile and makes a good accompaniment to most spiced dishes. It is especially suitable to serve with very hot food, as it has a deliciously cooling effect on the palate.*

**SERVES 2–4**

INGREDIENTS
*300 ml/¹/₂ pint/1¹/₄ cups natural (plain) yogurt*
*120 ml/4 fl oz/¹/₂ cup water*
*1 tsp salt*
*1 tbsp chopped fresh mint*
*2 tbsp chopped fresh coriander (cilantro)*
*1 fresh green chilli, chopped*
*cucumber slices*
*mint sprigs*

1  Whisk the yogurt in a mixing bowl.

2  Pour in the water and whisk again to thin down the yogurt slightly.

**3 ▲** Add the salt, fresh mint and coriander (cilantro) and chilli, and mix again.

**4 ▲** Transfer the raita into a serving dish, and garnish with cucumber slices and sprigs of mint.

# Fried Rice with Cashew Nuts

*Butter or ghee give the best flavour to fried rice, but you could also use corn oil if you prefer.*

**SERVES 4–6**

INGREDIENTS
*450 g/1 lb/2¹/₃ cups basmati rice*
*25 g/1 oz/2 tbsp unsalted butter or ghee*
*¹/₂ tsp onion seeds*
*3–4 curry leaves*
*1 medium onion, chopped*
*50 g/2 oz/¹/₂ cup cashew nuts*
*1 tsp salt*
*1 litre/1³/₄ pints/4 cups water*
*1 tbsp chopped fresh coriander (cilantro)*

1  Wash the rice twice, drain and set aside in a sieve (strainer).

**2 ▲** Melt the butter or ghee in a medium saucepan and fry the onion seeds and curry leaves for about 1 minute. Add the onion and stir-fry until golden brown.

3  Throw in the cashew nuts and salt, and fry for a few seconds.

**4 ▲** Add the rice and stir-fry for 1 minute, stirring gently. Pour in the water and fresh coriander (cilantro), and bring to the boil. Lower the heat, cover the pan with a tightly fitting lid and simmer for about 20 minutes.

5  Turn off the heat and leave the rice to stand, still covered, for about 5 minutes before serving.

*Raita (top) and Fried Rice with Cashew Nuts*

# Apricot Chutney

*Chutneys can add zest to most meals, and in Pakistan you will usually find a selection of different kinds served in tiny bowls for people to choose from. Dried apricots are readily available from supermarkets or health food shops.*

**MAKES ABOUT 450 g/1 lb**

**INGREDIENTS**

*450 g/1 lb/3 cups dried apricots, finely diced*
*1 tsp garam masala*
*275 g/10 oz/1¼ cups soft light brown sugar*
*450 ml/¾ pint/scant 2 cups malt vinegar*
*1 tsp ginger pulp*
*1 tsp salt*
*75 g/3 oz/½ cup sultanas (golden raisins)*
*450 ml/¾ pint/scant 2 cups water*

1 ▲ Put all the ingredients into a medium saucepan and mix together thoroughly.

2 ▲ Bring to the boil, then turn down the heat and simmer for 30–35 minutes, stirring occasionally.

3 When the chutney has thickened to a fairly stiff consistency, transfer into 2–3 clean jam jars and leave to cool. This chutney should be stored in the refrigerator.

# Tasty Toasts

*These crunchy toasts make an ideal snack or part of a brunch. They are especially delicious served with grilled (broiled) tomatoes and baked beans.*

**MAKES 4**

**INGREDIENTS**

*4 eggs*
*300 ml/½ pint/1¼ cups milk*
*2 fresh green chillies, finely chopped*
*2 tbsp chopped fresh coriander (cilantro)*
*75 g/3 oz/¾ cup Cheddar or mozzarella cheese, grated*
*½ tsp salt*
*¼ tsp freshly ground black pepper*
*4 slices bread*
*corn oil for frying*

1 Break the eggs into a medium bowl and whisk together. Slowly add the milk and whisk again. Add the chillies, coriander (cilantro), cheese, salt and pepper.

2 Cut the bread slices in half diagonally, and soak them, one at a time, in the egg mixture.

3 ▼ Heat the oil in a medium frying pan (skillet) and fry the bread slices over a medium heat, turning them once or twice, until they are golden brown.

4 Drain off any excess oil as you remove the toasts from the pan and serve immediately.

*Apricot Chutney (top) and Tasty Toasts*

# Index